Modern Critical Views

Edward Albee
Maya Angelou
Asian-American
  Writers
Margaret Atwood
Jane Austen
James Baldwin
Samuel Beckett
Saul Bellow
The Bible
William Blake
Jorge Luis Borges
Ray Bradbury
The Brontës
Gwendolyn Brooks
Robert Browning
Italo Calvino
Albert Camus
Lewis Carroll
Willa Cather
Cervantes
Geoffrey Chaucer
Anton Chekhov
Kate Chopin
Agatha Christie
Samuel Taylor
  Coleridge
Joseph Conrad
Contemporary Poets
Stephen Crane
Dante
Daniel Defoe
Charles Dickens
Emily Dickinson
John Donne and the
  17th-Century
  Poets
Fyodor Dostoevsky
W. E. B. DuBois
George Eliot
T. S. Eliot
Ralph Ellison
Ralph Waldo
  Emerson
William Faulkner
F. Scott Fitzgerald

Sigmund Freud
Robert Frost
George Gordon,
  Lord Byron
Graham Greene
Thomas Hardy
Nathaniel
  Hawthorne
Ernest Hemingway
Hispanic-American
  Writers
Homer
Langston Hughes
Zora Neale Hurston
Henrik Ibsen
John Irving
Henry James
James Joyce
Franz Kafka
John Keats
Jamaica Kincaid
Stephen King
Rudyard Kipling
D. H. Lawrence
Ursula K. Le Guin
Sinclair Lewis
Bernard Malamud
Christopher Marlowe
Gabriel García
  Márquez
Carson McCullers
Herman Melville
Arthur Miller
John Milton
Toni Morrison
Native-American
  Writers
Joyce Carol Oates
Flannery O'Connor
Eugene O'Neill
George Orwell
Sylvia Plath
Edgar Allan Poe
Katherine Anne
  Porter
J. D. Salinger

Jean-Paul Sartre
William Shakespeare:
  Histories and
  Poems
William Shakespeare's
  Romances
William Shakespeare:
  The Comedies
William Shakespeare:
  The Tragedies
George Bernard
  Shaw
Mary Wollstonecraft
  Shelley
Percy Bysshe Shelley
Alexander
  Solzhenitsyn
Sophocles
John Steinbeck
Tom Stoppard
Jonathan Swift
Amy Tan
Alfred, Lord
  Tennyson
Henry David
  Thoreau
J. R. R. Tolkien
Leo Tolstoy
Mark Twain
John Updike
Kurt Vonnegut
Alice Walker
Robert Penn Warren
Eudora Welty
Edith Wharton
Walt Whitman
Oscar Wilde
Tennessee Williams
Thomas Wolfe
Tom Wolfe
Virginia Woolf
William Wordsworth
Richard Wright
William Butler Yeats

Modern Critical Views

KURT VONNEGUT

Edited and with an introduction by
Harold Bloom
Sterling Professor of the Humanities
Yale University

CHELSEA HOUSE PUBLISHERS
Philadelphia

© 2000 by Chelsea House Publishers, a subsidiary of
Haights Cross Communications.

Introduction © 2000 by Harold Bloom

Printed and bound in the United States of America

10 9 8 7 6 5 4 3 2

∞ The paper used in this publication meets the minimum
requirements of the American National Standard for
Permanence of Paper for Printed Library Materials,
Z39.48-1984

Library of Congress Cataloging-in-Publication Data

Kurt Vonnegut / edited and with an introduction by Harold
Bloom.
        p . cm — (Modern critical views)
    Includes bibliographical references and index.
    ISBN 0-7910-5655-4 (alk. paper)
    1. Vonnegut, Kurt—Criticism and interpretation.
  2. Science fiction, American—History and criticism.
  I. Bloom, Harold.   II. Series.
  PS3572.O5 Z753   2000
  813'.54—dc21
                                    99-049119
                                         CIP

Contributing Editor: Tenley Williams

Contents

Editor's Note

My Introduction is an appreciation of *Slaughterhouse-Five*, neither Vonnegut's best novel (*Cat's Cradle*) nor his most disturbing (*Mother Night*) but probably his central and representative work.

Leonard Mustazza, who seems to me Vonnegut's most comprehensive exegete, analyzes the system of illusions that constitute *The Sirens of Titan*, and then concludes that Vonnegut wishes us to see ourselves in the dreadful figure of Howard Campbell, in *Mother Night*.

John L. Simons, explaining the playful complexities of *Cat's Cradle*, finds a Dostoevskian quality in the tragic philosophy of Bokononism, after which Leonard Mustazza returns to find a vision of Eden in the mental hospital of *God Bless You, Mr. Rosewater*.

Charles Berryman meditates upon Vonnegut's hilarious self-parody in *Breakfast of Champions*, while Peter Freese admires the skill with which Vonnegut conveys the atrocity memorialized in *Slaughterhouse-Five*, so as to allow the terror to break through our defenses.

Céline, perhaps the major influence upon Vonnegut, is judged by Philip Watts to have placed Vonnegut, particularly in *Slaughterhouse-Five*, in a "web of reimbursement," made more intricate by Céline's anti-Semitism.

Shamanism, the pragmatic religion of Vonnegut's fiction, is traced throughout his work by Lawrence R. Broer, while the *alter ego* of Vonnegut-as-author, Kilgore Trout, is analyzed by Peter J. Reed.

Vonnegut's return to fantasy in *Galápagos* and *Bluebird* is described by Donald E. Morse, after which Oliver W. Ferguson presents a fuller account of *Galápagos*.

Introduction

On December 19, 1944, Kurt Vonnegut was captured by the Germans during the Battle of the Bulge; he was twenty-two years old. Sent to Dresden, he survived the firebombing of the city on February 13–14, 1945, in which 135,000 Germans were killed. That is the biographical context (in part) for the novel, *Slaughterhouse-Five; or The Children's Crusade* (1969).

Since Vonnegut had begun publishing novels in 1952, it is clear that nearly a quarter-century had to go by before the trauma of 1945 could be transmuted into the exorcism of *Slaughterhouse-Five*. I have just reread the novel after thirty years, remembering my shocked admiration for it when it first appeared, and not looking forward to encountering it again. As it should, *Slaughterhouse-Five* remains a very disturbed and disturbing book, and still moves me to troubled admiration. I prefer *Cat's Cradle*, but *Slaughterhouse-Five* may prove to be an equally permanent achievement.

The shadow of Céline's *Journey to the End of the Night* never quite leaves Vonnegut's starker works, including *Slaughterhouse-Five*. I myself read the anti-Semitic Céline with loathing; one sees what is strong in the writing, but a Jewish literary critic is hardly Céline's ideal audience. So it goes.

It is difficult to comment upon *Slaughterhouse-Five* without being contaminated by its styles and procedures, which is necessarily a tribute to the book. In "structure" (an absurd term to apply to almost any novel by Vonnegut), *Slaughterhouse-Five* is a whirling medley, and yet it all coheres. Billy Pilgrim, as a character, does not cohere, but that is appropriate, since his schizophrenia (to call it that) is central to the book.

The planet Tralfamadore, where Billy enjoys pneumatic bliss with Montana Wildhack, is certainly preferable to a world of Nazi death camps and Dresden firebombings. The small miracle of *Slaughterhouse-Five* is that it could be composed at all. Vonnegut always writes from the survivor's stance, where all laughter has to be a step away from madness or fury. So indeed it goes.

1

Somewhere in the book, the Tralfamadorians tell Billy Pilgrim that their flying-saucer crews had verified the presence of seven sexes on Earth, all of them necessary if babies are to go on being born. I think that is one of the useful moral observations I will keep in mind whenever I recall *Slaughterhouse-Five*.

LEONARD MUSTAZZA

The Sirens of Titan *and the "Paradise Within"*

In his great etiological epic, *Paradise Lost,* John Milton departs in a number of ways from his source in Genesis. One of the most significant differences has to do with narrative point of view. Whereas the details about humanity before, during, and after the Fall rest completely upon surface matters in Genesis, Milton continually probes inner territory, so to speak, exposing the reader to what his characters are thinking and feeling, and suggesting, in the words of Satan, that "the mind is its own place, and in itself / Can make a Heav'n of Hell, a Hell of Heav'n." Indeed, the poem comes to rest precisely upon this theme of "inwardness." In the last two books, the Archangel Michael, carrying out his divine charge to expel Adam and Eve from Paradise, prefaces his action by giving Adam a preview of some scenes from the fallen world that he and Eve are about to enter—the murder of one of his sons by another, the frightening "Lazar-house . . . wherein were laid / Number of all diseas'd, all maladies," God's destruction of the earth by flood because of the evils of humanity, and, ultimately, the coming of the Messiah into the world to redeem it. Then, just prior to the actual expulsion from the Garden of Eden, Michael draws out the moral of all that he has shown to Adam, a moral that, in effect, contains all the wisdom necessary for life in the fallen world:

From *Forever Pursuing Genesis: The Myth of Eden in the Novels of Kurt Vonnegut* by Leonard Mustazza. © 1990 by Associated University Presses, Inc.

3

> This having learnt, thou hast attain'd the sum
> Of wisdom; hope no higher. Though all the Stars
> Thou knew'st by name, and all th'ethereal Powers,
> All secrets of the deep, all Nature's works,
> Or works of God in Heav'n, Air, Earth, or Sea,
> And all the riches of this World enjoy'dst,
> And all the rule, one Empire; only add
> Deeds to thy knowledge answerable, add Faith,
> Add Virtue, Patience, Temperance, add Love,
> By name to come call'd Charity, the soul
> Of all the rest; then thou wilt not be loath
> To leave this Paradise, but shalt possess
> A paradise within thee, happier far.

Knowledge, wealth, and political power, Michael advises, will not bring them happiness. The "paradise within" is a garden sown with seeds of virtue—chief among those virtues, love.

Now if we apply this Miltonic dichotomy between internal and external paradises to Vonnegut's *The Sirens of Titan*, we will notice some remarkable thematic similarities despite the obvious and vast differences that separate the two writers. From the very beginning, Vonnegut presents—indeed, he predicates his story upon—a similarly dichotomous view of internal and external circumstances:

> Everyone now knows how to find the meaning of life within himself.
>
> But mankind wasn't always so lucky. Less than a century ago men and women did not have easy access to the puzzle boxes within them.
>
> They could not name even one of the fifty-three portals to the soul.
>
> Gimcrack religions were big business.
>
> Mankind, ignorant of the truths that lie within every human being, looked outward—pushed ever outward. What mankind hoped to learn in its outward push was who was actually in charge of all creation, and what all creation was all about.
>
> Mankind flung its advance agents ever outward, ever outward. Eventually it flung them out into space, into the colorless, tasteless, weightless sea of outwardness without end.
>
> It flung them like stones.

These unhappy agents found what had already been found in abundance on Earth—a nightmare of meaninglessness without end. The bounties of space of infinite outwardness, were three: empty heroics, low comedy, and pointless death.

Outwardness lost, at last, its imagined attractions.

Only inwardness remained to be explored.

Only the human soul remained *terra incognita*.

This was the beginning of goodness and wisdom.

Although Vonnegut does not specify here the nature of the goodness and wisdom to be found within, we will come to discover that it is precisely the one that Milton calls "the soul / Of all the rest"—love. The journey into morally empty space, which most of the narrative concerns, will culminate in this discovery by the protagonist, Malachi Constant, who, significantly, is one of the richest and most powerful men in the world at the beginning of the novel (compare Michael's admonition to Adam above). Malachi, along with his mate, Beatrice, and their son, Chrono, will find the wisdom and goodness of love after they have taken up residence on an Edenic Titan, far from the troubled—fallen—world as we know it. In effect, they discover what Milton calls "the paradise within."

As is the case in many of Vonnegut's novels (notably *Slaughterhouse-Five* and *Galápagos*), the movement towards an Eden of sorts begins with its antithesis, the fallen world. The world into which the enigmatic Winston Niles Rumfoord periodically materializes is quite troubled, and the primary cause of its trouble, Vonnegut is careful to point out, has to do with the spiritual alienation of the species, the sense that life is without inherent meaning colliding with the desperate belief that there must be some source of meaning "out there" somewhere. Richard Giannone views the people here as living in a state of "moral dispossession," and he appropriately cites as the archetypal parable of such dispossession the Genesis account of Adam and Eve's expulsion from Eden. The evidence for this view is clear enough. Outside the Rumfoord estate on the day of one of his materializations, for instance, there is a crowd which, although denied admittance, has nevertheless gathered in the hopes of witnessing the "miracle" and perhaps even hearing from the semi-divine Rumfoord himself. Frustrated in their attempts, the crowd eventually begins a riot, which the narrator symbolically identifies as "an exercise in science and theology—a seeking after clues by the living as to what life was all about." Of course, according to the crowd's logic, only someone like Rumfoord, who communes constantly with the "up there," can supply such answers. The problem, however, is that Rumfoord is no more willing than the traditional deity he represents in their minds to supply direct answers.

Significantly, though, Rumfoord denies the connection between himself and God. "He never gave in to the temptation to declare himself God or something a whole lot like God," the narrator tells us. Declarations, however, are relatively meaningless; and there is no denying that the people look upon him as such a figure and, for all practical purposes, he plays precisely that role. To begin with, there is Rumfoord's anomalous existence itself. Having flown his private spaceship into a *chrono-synclastic infundibulum*, defined as one of the places "where all the different kinds of truths fit together," he exists now as a wave phenomenon that materializes on earth only at fixed intervals, the miraculous materializations that people there so avidly await. More importantly, at the same time that he lost his physical substantiality, he gained certain extraordinary talents, including the ability to read minds and to see into the future. He does not hesitate to use these talents in his self-appointed mission to reorder human priorities and thus save humankind from meaninglessness. That salvation will depend upon Rumfoord's secretive manipulation of two conceptual forms that have traditionally united divided people through the centuries—politics and religion. His plan includes two parts—an orchestrated "Martian" attack upon the earth and then his establishment of the Church of God of the Utterly Indifferent—both parts involving his shamelessly taking control over matters of life and death.

Despite the good he purports to serve with his plan, Rumfoord's god-playing is perhaps the most problematical moral issue in the novel as evidenced by the range of critical responses to it. Stanley Schatt has argued that "the millionaire is motivated by a selfish reason, basically a psychological need to change his society," and even his church is selfishly designed "because he cannot tolerate the thought that he does not control his own destiny." Likewise, Russell Blackford maintains that "Vonnegut uses every imaginable device to show us Rumfoord's unreliability. Rumfoord is often manipulative, deceitful, or mistaken; his words should never be granted at their face value." On the other hand, G. K. Wolfe writes that Rumfoord "realizes that the only hope for man lies in a complete restructuring of society, and he hopes to bring about this restructuring." Peter Scholl, admitting that Rumfoord is part tyrant and part charlatan, also considers his establishment of a religion a good thing since it "eliminates national boundaries and makes warfare a thing of the past." David Goldsmith regards Rumfoord's intentions as a bit cynical but essentially sincere: "He is out to prove to the inhabitants of Earth that their religions are useless and myopic, while his at least has the benefit of being headed by someone who can see into the future." Joseph Sigman, finally, notes that Rumfoord, far from being anything like a deity, is really "a parody of a deity," and through him Vonnegut parodies the entire idea of a divine consciousness as an absolute frame of reference providing a basis for truth and objectivity.

All of these critical assessments are valid to one extent or another, and yet none of them takes into account the ironic element that Vonnegut builds into this characterization. As artist, Vonnegut could have chosen to make his wave-phenomenon character virtually anyone, but he deliberately chooses a very wealthy, well-bred, snobbish man for this role. That he is a person of old wealth—as directly opposed to the *nouveau-riche* Malachi Constant—is significant in terms of the attitudes toward life, toward his own worth, and toward other people that Rumfoord holds. On a small scale, we first see these attitudes revealed in a conversation with Malachi near the beginning of the novel. At one point, the conversation turns to the topic of Malachi's wealth:

> "They tell me you are possibly the luckiest man who ever lived."
>
> "That might be putting it a little too strong," said Constant.
>
> "You won't deny that you've had fantastically good luck financially," said Rumfoord.
>
> Constant shook his head. "No. That would be hard to deny," he said.
>
> "And to what do you attribute this wonderful luck of yours?" said Rumfoord.
>
> Constant shrugged. "Who knows?" he said. "I guess somebody up there likes me," he said.
>
> Rumfoord looked up at the ceiling. "What a charming concept—someone's liking you up there."
>
> Constant, who had been shaking hands with Rumfoord during the conversation, thought of his own hand, suddenly, as small and clawlike.

Constant is, to be sure, a perceptive man. He immediately feels diminished to precisely the degree that Rumfoord intends; and given Rumfoord's harsh manipulation of Malachi's fate later in the novel, we must conclude that this ego assault was quite deliberate. His lack of regard and sensitivity for this man is clearly carried over to his view of the unwashed masses assembled outside his door. Is it any wonder, then, that his plan for the salvation of the species includes the deaths of so many people? Indeed, it is small wonder that he sets himself up as the disposer of people's lives. Feelings are unimportant to Rumfoord, and people are expendable. The experiment is all.

For this reason, we come to regard Rumfoord's intellectual defeat in the end as an exercise in poetic justice. Our antipathy for him begins when we recognize the contours of his grand political plan beginning with the Martian attack upon earth. Of course, his "Martians" are really "Earthlings" whom Rumfoord has had kidnapped and mentally programmed to obey. The programming involves the removal of their ability to think, feel, and remember. Using these people to launch his planned attack, Rumfoord sees to it that the "Earthlings" unify themselves against the common enemy, most of whom they slaughter. The fact that what they are doing is actually slaughtering their own kind makes no difference to Rumfoord. All that matters is the grand effect he has achieved, the success of the experiment. He congratulates himself on a plan well executed (pun intended), though, like a true politician and patrician elitist, he carefully guards the secrets of the plan from the loyal victors lest they get the wrong idea of his moral scruples and his designs for them.

Indeed, the second phase of his unification plan, the religious phase, does involve these "victors," and again Rumfoord employs here concealment, half-truths, illusion, victimization, and, of course, dazzling spectacle, which Vonnegut reduces to a kind of side show, replete with a carnival barker, Marlin T. Lapp, who works the crowd, preparing them for the "things in the Universe as yet undreamed of" that they are about to learn. Rumfoord then materializes to his worshipping masses and delivers a speech to inaugurate the new religion he has devised, the Church of God of the Utterly Indifferent. Not surprisingly, the speech itself is egotistical and self-serving, designed primarily to magnify his own name. Altruism, though seemingly his motive for action, is the last thing on Rumfoord's mind. Here is the general movement of the speech:

1. He reveals that the doomed Martians were really Earthlings who, he claims, died gladly in order that the people of Earth might at last become one family—joyful, fraternal, and proud.
2. He says that the time is now ripe for national borders, along with the lust for war, fear, and hatred, to disappear.
3. He announces the principal teachings of his new church: "Puny man can do nothing at all to help or please God Almighty, and Luck is not the hand of God."
4. He strongly advises them to subscribe to the new religion "because I, as head of this religion, can work miracles, and the head of no other religion can. . . . I can work the miracle of predicting, with absolute accuracy, the things that the future will bring."

5. In the manner of Christ's Sermon on the Mount, he tells a parable about Malachi Constant and luck.

6. As he is about to disappear, he promises to bring them a new Bible the next time he materializes, a Bible "revised so as to be meaningful in modern times.

Keeping to his promise, he does appear again, in an even more spectacular performance, bringing to the crowd the messianic Unk to preach the gospel of luck and Malachi Constant, who has now become the personification of the former ills of the world and who must be sacrificed for the good of humanity. What is significant about these messiah and pariah figures, of course, is that they are one and the same man, whom Rumfoord has unscrupulously used for the advancement of his ends. In an ironic version of the Sermon on the Mount, Rumfoord delivers his diatribe against his invented symbolic version of Malachi Constant from up in a tree, and then he informs Malachi that he, along with Rumfoord's own wife, Beatrice, and the child born of the union of Beatrice and Malachi, Chrono, will be banished to Titan, a warm and fecund moon of Saturn. The three of them, Rumfoord decrees, will live there in safety and comfort, though in exile from their native earth, and the purpose of this banishment is "so that the Church of God of the Utterly Indifferent can have a drama of dignified self-sacrifice to remember and ponder through all time."

Now if one attends carefully to all that Rumfoord says in these carefully modulated speeches, his motives for action become quite clear—motives that give the lie to his denials of aspiration to godhead and, hence, that sharply undercut the arguments of those critics who see any traces of altruism in his plans. In the first speech, summarized above, we hear him lie to his future congregation about the reasons the Earthling-Martians gave up their lives. They did not, in fact, die willingly to unify the earth; rather, Rumfoord sacrificed them for that announced purpose. We also hear him make the untenable claim that this bit of space-opera spectacle can have the effect of eliminating inherent human feelings (envy, hatred, fear), along with national boundaries. He also sees to it that they handicap themselves with weights and other devices meant to hamper natural human advantages. In effect, Rumfoord wants nothing less than to remake the human species, not in his own image, for he will remain superior and unhandicapped, but in an image that he considers good. That he has to sacrifice people's lives to do it, that he has to eliminate natural and often beneficial advantages to level out distinctions, that he has to turn people into unthinking automata are unimportant to him. After all, he regards himself, despite his denials to the contrary, as a god as evidenced by his boast that no other religion has as its head a miracle worker, an obvious swipe at Christianity. And, to top off his aspirations and his disdain for conventional religions, notably Christianity, he promises to give them a revised Bible; one, no doubt, that will magnify his own works.

As I suggested earlier, it is no mere coincidence that Vonnegut places his protagonist in this novel, Malachi Constant, in a position that is both similar to and vastly different from Rumfoord's. He, too, is a fabulously wealthy and powerful American. His wealth and power have been due to luck, and that fact seems to disturb the patrician, old-monied Rumfoord a great deal, though he fails to acknowledge that his own wealth, however time honored, was acquired in much the same way as Malachi's through an accident of birth. Nevertheless, seeming to display *noblesse oblige*, he reveals his disdain for the ingenuous Malachi; and one is led to suspect strongly that his choice of Malachi as a sacrificial symbol is motivated by a good bit of malice. For his part, Malachi, despite his enviable position, is really not much different from other people. Like them, he is seeking the meaning of life, and Rumfoord promises to deliver it to him, though he does so in a self-serving truncated form, and in a mythically symbolic gesture. Appearing in a foyer of his mansion, where there is a mosaic floor showing the signs of the zodiac around a golden sun, the god-player symbolically "stands on the sun" and makes his wondrous predictions: that Malachi will mate with Rumfoord's frigid and aristocratic wife, Beatrice, on Mars, that she will have a son named Chrono, and that they will all eventually be united on Titan. At first "Malachi Constant of Hollywood" opposes "Winston Niles Rumfoord of Newport and Eternity," but eventually considers the plan quite agreeable. In fact, it becomes so appealing to him that, when Beatrice later calls her husband insane, Malachi defends the prediction, claiming that he himself already possesses the means for such space travel, a space ship called *The Whale*. Of course, as we soon learn, Malachi's defense of Rumfoord is premature for he has not been told the half of what Rumfoord has in store for him.

David Goldsmith has argued that *The Sirens of Titan* is, by authorial design, only ostensibly about the conflict between Rumfoord and Constant, but "the opponent here is none other than God himself." "Does anybody up there like us?" Goldsmith continues. "Is there anybody up there at all? Are those who are manipulating us here on earth in turn being manipulated by higher powers? Vonnegut's answers to all these questions is a firm, but not nihilistic no." I disagree with this assessment. I think the novel's meaning lies precisely in the conflict between these two characters and that, except in the most general terms, *The Sirens of Titan* is really no more about religion than it is about science fiction, both of these being devices to define sources of meaning, the intellectual and the environmental. For the reader, the God of Judeo-Christian tradition is relevant here only as a conventional standard against which to measure Rumfoord's qualities (for example, his inscrutability, his desire for worship and obedience) and his aspirations as a creator (that is, his making of a world in an image he deems good). Against this character's lofty goals we see Malachi, a man who is used by the other, a man who gets the reader's sympathy precisely because, in comparison to the other, he is humble and ingenuous, a man whose ultimate happiness we are pleased about, just as we are pleased with the eventual undoing of the great god Rumfoord.

Indeed, Rumfoord's ultimate disappointment will underscore for the reader the fact that ego and not altruism motivated his grand gestures. Two events bring on this disappointment. The first has to do with Rumfoord's displacement from this solar system owing to an explosion on the sun, a cause which is surely meant to recall ironically his positioning earlier when he stood on the mosaic sun in his foyer arrogantly making predictions to Malachi. This displacement, moreover, will involve his separation from his faithful dog, Kazak, another fact that causes him distress. "A Universe schemed in mercy," the narrator concludes, "would have kept man and dog together." But the universe, as everyone in the novel has discovered, is not schemed in mercy, not on a grand scale anyway, and no one is in a better position to acknowledge this truth than Winston Niles Rumfoord himself— after all, he is the founder of the Church of God of the Utterly Indifferent and the architect of a scheme that involved the merciless sacrifice of thousands. And yet he is embittered by his forced separation from his dog and his loss of control over his destiny and, by implication, the destinies of the people of earth. Within this context, the narrator's comment cited above cannot fail to strike the reader as humorously ironic.

Even more ironic is Rumfoord's resentment over what he perceives as a betrayal by one of his extraterrestrial cohorts. All along, we discover, Rumfoord has been aided in his schemes by Salo, a robotic creature from the planet Tralfamadore, who had been delivering a message when his spaceship broke down on Titan. The replacement part that the Tralfamadorians eventually send him turns out to be a piece of metal that Chrono, Malachi and Beatrice's son, carries around as his good luck piece. In other words, while Rumfoord thought that he was controlling the destinies of human beings on Earth and, on a smaller scale, the lives of Malachi and Beatrice, it was actually he who was being controlled by the Tralfamadorians to deliver the replacement part. That realization is a bitter pill for Rumfoord to swallow, and he takes his frustration out on the kindly robot, complaining that the Tralfamadorians have "reached into the Solar System, picked me up, and used me like a handy-dandy potato peeler!" Then, hardly able to maintain his usual pose of *noblesse oblige*, he tells Salo, "It may surprise you to learn that I take a certain pride, no matter how foolishly mistaken that pride may be, in making my own decisions for my own reasons." Of course he takes such pride while he has seen fit to deny others the pride of making their own decisions. Continually flaunting his wealth and good breeding, continually trying to impress people with his spectacles of power, continually lecturing others in his "glottal Groton tenor," Rumfoord has been content to manage human affairs by virtue of nothing more than his own sense of self-worth, a kind of social Darwinism at its very worst. I said earlier that Vonnegut deliberately chose to make this utopian schemer a man from the social elite (and an elitist), and that choice turns out to be as much a satiric commentary on the cold arrogance of class-conscious America as it is a swipe at large-scale utopian schemes themselves.

As for Vonnegut's other wealthy American, Malachi Constant, the author reserves a different sort of fate for him, a kinder one, and there, too, we see the working out of yet another kind of poetic justice. For all of his life, Malachi has been both blessed and victimized by luck or chance. First he inherited his three-billion-dollar fortune from his father, Noel, who made the money through blind luck playing the stock market by using the initials of corporations that coincided with the first lines of the Bible. He died, we learn, by the time he reached the creation of light in Genesis. Then, after his meeting with Rumfoord, Malachi's luck changes. He loses his entire fortune and is subsequently used by Rumfoord as a pawn in the latter's schemes for world unification. In the end, finally, he finds happiness on Titan with his mate and his son: he will learn to deliver, in James Mellard's words, "the only message that we have to deliver—a life." In effect, Malachi will discover an Edenic place and, more important, what Milton would call "the paradise within." This latter discovery allows him to find what he went to Rumfoord to find in the first place—the meaning of life, which is to take charge of our lives whenever we can and to love others. Significantly, moreover, Vonnegut allows Malachi, along with his equally abused son and mate, to discover the internal paradise of meaning at the same time that Rumfoord, the great "tribal god," discovers the failure of his own external paradise on earth.

As for the external paradise that Malachi and his family find on Titan, Vonnegut never explicitly calls it Eden, and yet it is quite clear that this fictional place is meant to summon up visions of an Edenic locus and way of life. Unlike the noxious atmosphere of Mars, Titan is rich in oxygen and redolent, in the narrator's words, "like the atmosphere outside the back door of an Earthling bakery on a spring morning." Spring-like, too, is its climate; the temperature on the moon remains a constant sixty-five degrees

Fahrenheit. Moreover, the place is graced with a variety of natural wonders, including lovely rivers, lakes, and streams (all of which Rumfoord has egotistically named after himself and his dog, Kazak) and a view of "the most appallingly beautiful things in the Solar System, the rings of Saturn" (also egotistically named "Rumfoord's Rainbow"). In short, Titan is, according to one critic, a place where "primitive union with nature and simple pastoral dignity are chosen as forms of escape from fascist authoritarianism." In other words, it is something remarkably like Eden.

What is more, the new inhabitants of this Edenic Titan, freed from the arrogant tyrant they were forced to serve, find much more than pastoral simplicity and dignity. They find within themselves the meaning, peace, and contentment that they were lacking in their erstwhile "privileged" lives on earth. Beatrice Rumfoord, whose name Clark Mayo calls a "Dantean pun [since] Bee is more bitch than vision of loveliness," turns out to be much more dignified and even lovely than this interpretation suggests. "To anyone with a sense of poetry, morality, and wonder," the narrator tells us, "Malachi Constant's proud, high-cheekboned mate was a handsome as a human being could be." More important, she displays inner handsomeness as well. Most of her time in her declining years is spent writing a book, *The True Purpose of Life in the Solar System*. That she does so "on a moon with only two people on it" is immaterial, for the writing is not the communal act we call art but rather an existential assertion. Her thesis: to deny that free will is impossible given the manipulation of Earthlings by the forces of Tralfamadore. Despite the fact that the people of earth have unwittingly been made to serve the Tralfamadorians' interests, she maintains they have done so "in such highly personalized ways that Tralfamadore can be said to have had practically nothing to do with the case." In other words, she defines free will not as the ability to make endless choices, but to make choices whenever we can; and even if we are unknowingly carrying out the will of some great power (the Tralfamadorians, Rumfoord, even God), we are nevertheless free in the choice of our way to do it. Besides, she later maintains, "the worst thing that could possibly happen to anybody would be not to be used for anything by anybody." That Vonnegut is making this particular point the thesis of this novel about free will is, I think, dubious. Rather, it is Beatrice's act of assertion that gives her the dignity and meaning that she wants; and to a large extent in Vonnegut's world, we are what we do or say or even pretend to be.

As for Chrono, Malachi and Beatrice's surly and unsociable son, he, too, finds happiness on Titan, not in the company of his parents or in the verbal assertion of his freedom, but among the Titanic bluebirds, the creatures the book calls "the most admirable" on Titan and that proverbial wisdom associates with happiness. Moreover, Chrono has also found religion after his fashion. He spends a good deal of his time constructing stone shrines that symbolically represent Saturn and its nine moons, the one for Titan having under it a bluebird's feather. Perhaps the most impressive thing that Chrono does in the closing pages of the novel is to appear at his mother's funeral. He is, we are told, "gorgeous and strong," wearing a "feather cape which he flapped like wings." Accompanied by thousands of Titanic bluebirds, Chrono has come to bid farewell to his mother and to thank his parents for the gift of life. Several critics have remarked upon Chrono's remarkable transformation during his time on Titan. Peter Reed writes that, "from being a dishearteningly aggressive, cynical, and unfeeling boy, Chrono comes to align himself with the most beautiful creatures available and to appreciate the gift of life. . . . Chrono's appalling childhood has left him still able to praise . . . and that in the circumstances is no small wonder." S. A. Cowan sees the change in Chrono as one of the positive resolutions of the novel, a resolution that contrasts sharply with the lack of purpose felt by most of humanity throughout the work. Indeed, Chrono, like his mother, has changed; and we must attribute this change to the peaceful, isolated place they now inhabit, far from the madding crowd and beyond the reach of the grand schemer, Rumfoord.

Malachi Constant, finally, also finds happiness on Titan, a contentment that is much more complete and satisfying than anything he once enjoyed, even as the richest Earthling. Aging peacefully and gracefully, going about naked most of the time, Malachi learns in this paradisal place the value of love, both for his son and his mate. He is with Beatrice when she dies, and, in what is perhaps the most touching scene in the book, she thanks him for having used her, for bothering with her at all. After her death, Malachi will be left alone, but he will also be left with an important realization, which, in effect, constitutes the theme of *The Sirens of Titan*: that "a purpose of human life, no matter who is controlling it, is to love whoever is around to be loved."

Of course, there is a telling irony in the entire Titan episode. While Beatrice, Chrono, and Malachi do come to enjoy both a paradise without and within there, it is a paradise that involves, in Russell Blackford's words, "physical separation from their kind." In other words, it is only through forcible removal from the society of human beings that they achieve their contentment, and the implication here is that they would never have enjoyed anything like that sort of happiness had they remained on earth. To be sure, Paul Proteus dreamed of a similar form of escape; and as we shall see, almost every one of Vonnegut's protagonists who tries to construct a little Eden for himself envisions, so to speak, a limited sphere of operations, which includes a mate, a happy (often rural) environment away from the troubled world, and little else. Like these others Malachi Constant cannot enjoy his paradise once his mate is dead; and so, he accepts in the end the Tralfamadorian robot's offer to take him back to earth, where he will die a happy death because of the compassion shown him by Salo. That compassion again reveals Vonnegut's pervasive irony. The little robot, the machine that Rumfoord earlier accused of lacking feeling, hypnotizes Malachi so that, as he dies, he imagines that he sees his best friend, Stony Stevenson (whom he murdered while under Rumfoord's control), taking him to Paradise, where Beatrice awaits, where everyone is happy forever, or, as Stevenson qualifies matters, "as long as the bloody Universe holds together."

Peter Reed has likened Malachi's return to earth to "Prospero's leaving his magic island, to go back to his own kind." Though this analogy is provocative, it also distorts the matter, as all analogies do. Quite unlike the Shakespearean comic resolution, Vonnegut's endings always leave the reader uncomfortable, always suggest that what we are looking at is, at best, a compromise in a dire situation, and at worst, the maintenance of illusory hope in the face of existential hopelessness. Just as is the case when we watch Billy Pilgrim among the Tralfamadorians, moreover, we are made to see the full extent of the illusions that Malachi harbors; and, though we are glad for his happy death, we also know the truth that he does not. Both Billy and Malachi pursue Genesis after their fashion, and the illusion of having obtained an external Eden and the actual attainment of a "paradise within" is good enough for them. As one critic notes, "there are no green worlds" in Vonnegut's fiction, only the sustaining, sometimes life-giving illusions of such, and it is with these illusions of our own making that we must be content.

LEONARD MUSTAZZA

Das Reich der Zwei:
Art and Love as Miscreations in Mother Night

In the introduction added to *Mother Night* in 1966, some five years after its original publication, Vonnegut writes that this is the only story of his whose moral he knows. The main moral, he says, is that "we are what we pretend to be, so we must be careful about what we pretend to be"; and at the end of the introduction, he adds two other morals, almost as afterthoughts: that "when you're dead you're dead"; and that one should "make love when you can [because] it's good for you." These thematic announcements, for all their simplicity of articulation and facetiousness of tone, turn out to be accurate assessments of the novel's concerns. Indeed, *Mother Night*, the fictional autobiography of the erstwhile playwright, Nazi propagandist, and American spy Howard Campbell, Jr., is about nothing so much as pretense (political, artistic, and personal), death, and love. What we will also see is that the novel is an "only" in another sense as well, a sense that is not as specifically explicated as the story's morals; namely, that this is the only Vonnegut novel with an explicitly mythic title. In the Editor's Note, Vonnegut tells us that the title is Campbell's own and that it is taken from a speech by Mephistopheles in Goethe's *Faust*. That is the only explanation provided, and, curiously, not one reference to the mythic figure "Night," the daughter-consort of Chaos in classical mythology, occurs in the autobiography itself. Thus, we are left to sort out its significance on our own; and if we link the

From *Forever Pursuing Genesis: The Myth of Eden in the Novels of Kurt Vonnegut* by Leonard Mustazza. © 1990 by Associated University Presses, Inc.

title's possible meaning to the morals that Vonnegut does specify, we are left with the question how are pretense, death, and love associated with the primeval mythic personage referred to in the title? The answer to that question will be the subject of this chapter.

A good many writers of myth-based fictions, classical and biblical, have used "Night" to refer their readers to a time and condition prior to creation, which is often defined not in terms of making something out of nothing but rather as the imposition of form and order on chaotic matter. Both chaos and the ordered universe, moreover, literally apply to physical matter; but each condition also has moral implications as well, chaos representing the absence of a moral order and/or civilizing social influence. In works where "Night" is referred to, it is almost invariably the latter sense that is evoked. Moving in a mythically retrograde scheme, such works take us from an ordered condition back to a time prior to the imposition of a physical and moral order. In other words, in contrast to the creative process, that which is seen in backward-moving fiction represents an ironic miscreation.

One of the oldest literary accounts of Night is found in Hesiod's *Theogony* (ca. 700 B.C.), where primal Chaos (Void) and Night are seen as the progenitors of the passions, principles, and states of being that themselves precede the physical and moral order:

> First of all, the Void [Chaos, in Greek] came into being, next broad-bosomed Earth, the solid and eternal home of all, and Eros, the most beautiful of the immortal gods, who in every man and every god softens the sinews and overpowers the prudent purpose of the mind. Out of Void came Darkness and black Night, and out of Night came Light and Day, her children conceived after union in love with Darkness. . . .
>
> Night gave birth to hateful Destruction and the black Specter and Death; she also bore Sleep and the race of Dreams—all these the dark goddess Night bore without sleeping with any male. Next she gave birth to Blame and painful Grief, and also the Fates and the pitiless Specters of Vengeance. . . . Deadly Night also bore Retribution to plague men, then Deceit and Love and accursed Old Age and stubborn Strife.

As a unified etiological myth, the *Theogony* is, as Norman O. Brown writes in the introduction to his translation, a work that projects two dominant plans: "the historical process culminating in Zeus' supremacy over the divine cosmos, and the character of Zeus' rule." Put another way, it is concerned with the period immediately before and after the establishment of an ordered hierarchical cosmos.

The Judeo-Christian creation myth in Genesis, by contrast, is much less concerned with the question of matter and form prior to creation. In fact, very little is overtly said about the nature of pre-creation matter there, though the opening lines of Genesis do suggest the physical equivalents to the figures personified in the Greek account:

> In the beginning of Creation, when God made heaven and earth, the earth was without form and void, with darkness over the face of the abyss, and a mighty wind that swept over the surface of the waters (Genesis 1:1–2).

Thus, the formless void can be seen as the generic equivalent of the personified "Void" of the *Theogony*, and darkness stands for Hesiod's Night.

Indeed, so closely associated are these terms that many Christian writers have in their works blurred the distinctions between the Greek and the Judeo-Christian creation stories. John Milton, for instance, features Night and Chaos as the monarchical anarchs of the abyss that Satan travels through on his journey from Hell to God's newly created earth, which he spitefully hopes to mar however he can. Traveling through "the hollow dark," Satan at one point beholds

> the Throne
> Of *Chaos*, and his dark Pavilion spread
> Wide on the wasteful Deep; with him Enthron'd
> Sat sable-vested *Night*, eldest of things,
> The Consort of his Reign.
>
> (*Paradise Lost*)

Satan tells Chaos and his dark consort of his plan to spite God by ruining his creation, thus raising on earth "the Standard there of *ancient Night*," a plan that the old anarch immediately endorses since the ordered universe has sharply limited his territories, "Weak'ning the Sceptre of old *Night*." In effect, what Satan and Chaos are hoping for here is an undoing of creation, a miscreation that would allow the ancient forces of disorder and darkness to reestablish themselves.

Alexander Pope's neoclassical mock epic, *The Dunciad*, also employs Night and Chaos, albeit from a different perspective from Milton's. Satirizing the decline in artistic values and, more generally, of civilization in his own time, Pope casts his diatribe in terms of the mythic retrogression of the world, moving all the way back to the reestablishment of Chaos and Night's cosmic supremacy:

> In vain, in vain—the all-composing Hour
> Resistless falls: The Muse obeys the Pow'r.
> She comes! she comes! the sable Throne behold
> Of *Night* Primaeval, and of *Chaos* old!
> Before her, *Fancy's* gilded clouds decay,
> And all its varying Rain-bows die away.
>
> . . . .
>
> Thus at her felt approach, and secret might,
> *Art* after *Art* goes out, and all is Night.
>
> . . . .
>
> Lo! thy dread Empire, CHAOS! is restor'd;
> Light dies before thy uncreating word:
> Thy hand, great Anarch! lets the curtain fall;
> And Universal Darkness buries All.
>
> (*Dunciad*)

In both Milton's and Pope's visions, Night and Chaos represent not only the literal embodiments of the forces of miscreation, the "uncreating word," but also and most importantly moral and intellectual disorder as well.

Finally, there is the passage from Goethe's *Faust* that Vonnegut excerpts in the Editor's Note to *Mother Night*; and we find here again the same reverse movement employing Christianized classical figures. In this version, we hear Mephistopheles, associating his own purposes with those of Night, expressing the hope that "supercilious light," born of Night herself, will be destroyed, along with "the world's stuff," thus reaffirming the supreme cosmic status of Mother Night."

The concept of mythic backward movements and miscreations that all of these writers speak of can well be applied to Vonnegut's novel, even though Campbell never mentions Night in the autobiography itself, nor does the editor ever explicate the significance of Campbell's title. For his entire life, Campbell has been involved in nothing so much as attempting to create for himself a little universe, a limited sphere of operations in which he can enjoy order, beauty, light, and love. As an artist, he does what all artists do: he chooses things from the dark and chaotic material of life and creates "worlds." Like all artists, he exercises selective consciousness, so to speak, to make his little worlds; and, because his creations are plays, he is also able to watch as his worlds are brought vividly to life on the stage. For Vonnegut, such selective consciousness, whether in artistic creations or in life, represents a form of lying, particularly when it occurs within the context of the greater reality (chaos) of the world around us, replete with so many other remakers of their own worlds. And yet, he also admits in the Editor's Note to the novel that mendacious activities of this kind "can be, in a higher sense, the most beguiling forms of truth." *Mother Night*, however, is not concerned simply with the small, beguiling truths that one invents for oneself to survive happily. Rather, its main focus is the collision of one man's little world with those of potent others within the greater chaos; and in a more general and figurative sense, with the endless conflict between our own "supercilious lights" and the greater darkness. In many ways, it fulfills Mephistopheles's hope (or, for that matter, Satan's in *Paradise Lost*, or that of the forces of disorder in *The Dunciad*) that Mother Night's ancient reign be reestablished.

The process leading to Night's eventual victory begins just after Howard Campbell has put the finishing touches on his pleasant little world. Howard's recruitment by Frank Wirtanen (code named his "Blue Fairy Godmother") to serve as a Nazi propagandist and an American agent comes, therefore, at a thematically significant point in the narrative. This is how Howard recalls his thoughts prior to his encounter with Wirtanen in the Tiergarten in Berlin:

> I was sitting alone on a park bench in the sunshine that day, thinking of a fourth play that was beginning to write itself in my mind. It gave itself a title, which was *"Das Reich der Zwei"*—"Nation of Two."
>
> It was going to be about the love my wife and I had for each other. It was going to show how a pair of lovers in a world gone mad could survive by being loyal only to a nation composed of themselves—a nation of two.

This description draws together the two forms of escape that Howard was content to engage in—his art and his love for his wife, the latter related to the former not only in the subject matter of the play, but also because his wife, Helga Noth, is the principal actress in his productions. Jerome Klinkowitz has argued that the traditional retreats of art and love can be effective in providing solace if one has "a self to flee to, a self which cannot be reached and abused by others." Howard clearly has such a self at this point, as evidenced by his design to flee, if only in a limited sense, from the world's madness, and even later, after the death of his wife and his relocation to New York, we see him still fleeing into the self, in this case complete enclosure within the self. In other words, he makes personal choices for coping with the madness or chaos around him. While some choose political participation or social diversion, he chooses art and love and limited participation insofar as he agrees to cooperate with Wirtanen. Still, the world he makes for himself, his nation of two, is not so far-fetched that we cannot at least sympathize with the choice or even see it as quite desirable.

Curiously, however, Howard's choices have left him open to some of the most censuring commentary made on any of Vonnegut's protagonists. Stanley Schatt regards the artist Campbell as an unreliable narrator. "Since Campbell is not only the narrator of *Mother Night* but also a playwright," he argues, "an artist who uses his imagination to construct a more pleasant world, it is very difficult to determine what is real in his universe." Speaking of his uncommitted political views, Kathryn Hume reaches the same conclusion about his reliability: "The psychological split induced by conflicts of national loyalty and personal indifference to politics and responsibility add up to a schizoid imbalance so severe that readers do not trust him to be analytical or truthful." Apart from his politics, even his attitude toward love has led to sharp criticism. Clark Mayo sees his nation of two as an escape from social responsibility, as a "sensual rather than a metaphysical reality," and he concludes that Vonnegut is really endorsing "not the egocentric and community-denying 'Nation of Two,' but rather 'uncritical love.'" Likewise, William Veeder sees Howard's brand of love as a device to seal himself away from the rest of humanity, and he concludes that "even when the beloved is more than a mirror of the protagonist, romantic love can allow too complete an indulgence of the self."

What these commentators say is, of course, quite valid. And yet, even as we recognize the self-deceptions that Howard engages in, we also see in him something genuine and sincere. To be sure, he is often painfully honest about his inner reality—his feelings and perceptions of the world—and, seeing the world through his eyes even as we maintain our own political and personal perspectives on the events described, we are made, at once, to sympathize with his human desires and to criticize the excessiveness of his self-delusions. Howard possesses the same kind of pathetic naivete that, say, Billy Pilgrim or Rudy Waltz does, a self-limiting view of life. In other words, we have here a fairly typical Vonnegut perspective on life, a dual vision that allows us to recognize Howard's weaknesses and to sympathize with his escapist "solutions" because we all often seek escape of one kind or another. Thus, like most of Vonnegut's protagonists, particularly those he places in very stressful and uncontrollable situations like war or politics, Howard is seeking not to assess and cooperate in external circumstances but to escape from them however he can. Like his counterparts in other Vonnegut novels, Howard uses as a means of escape a mental construct that represents for him a re-creation of reality along familiar mythic lines.

The particular creation myth to which he subscribes is, as I suggested earlier, a well-known and conventional one that Vonnegut turns to again and again in his fictions: the story of Noah. Late in the novel, in a chapter entitled "No Dove, No Covenant," Howard briefly describes his life with Helga during the war, likening his feelings upon entering his New York apartment to those he experienced in Berlin many years before:

> The air was clean.
>
> The feeling of a stale old building suddenly laid open, an infected atmosphere lanced, made clean, was familiar to me. I had felt it often enough in Berlin. Helena and I were bombed out twice. Both times there was a staircase left to climb.
>
> One time we climbed the stairs to a roofless and windowless house, a house otherwise magically undisturbed. Another time, we climbed the stairs to cold thin air, two floors below where home had been.
>
> Both moments at those splintered stairheads under the open sky were exquisite.
>
> The exquisiteness went on for only a short time, naturally, for, like any human family, we loved our nests and needed them. But, for a minute or two, anyway, Helga and I felt like Noah and his wife on Mount Ararat.
>
> There is no better feeling than that.

This feeling does not and cannot last. They soon realized, he goes on, that "the flood, far from being over, had scarcely begun," that the menace of falling bombs proved to them that they "were ordinary people, without dove or covenant" to show their special status or their divine protection.

Richard Giannone has argued that Howard and Helga's figurative Noah's Ark represents a means of "surviv[ing] the flood of violent madness that is inundating the world" but that this world "has a way of shattering the idea retreats we construct in fancy." This interpretation of Vonnegut's reference to Noah is valid enough, but it is also too generally applied. If we attend carefully to Howard's reference, however, we notice that he is not equating his life to Noah's during the Flood, but rather to the periods before and after the great deluge. According to the account in Genesis, both periods are marked by widespread immorality. Prior to the Flood, Noah is the only blameless man left on earth amid the immorality that makes God, anthropomorphically represented as he is, repent of ever having made humankind (Genesis 6:7–9). Then, causing both a literal and symbolic miscreation of his own, God submerges the earth in water, thereby recalling, figuratively, the waters of chaos that he had dispersed at the creation. After the Flood, God effects through Noah and those creatures who accompanied him a re-creation of the earth, again both figuratively and literally in Genesis. The figurative re-creation is seen in the repetition of God's injunction that Noah and the others "Be fruitful and increase and fill the earth" (Genesis 9:1), an explicit repetition of the divine injunction to Adam and Eve (Genesis 1:28). Thus, the world upon which Noah looks is nearly as new and as fresh as the one Adam beheld upon awakening to life, though, unlike Adam, Noah will have little choice in the future course of humanity. Indeed, before long, the immorality that existed prior to the Flood will again take hold, and the writer(s) of Genesis shows this unhappy progression both within the account of Noah itself, with Noah cursing his son Canaan, and following it, with the story of the Tower of Babel.

Applying Noah's experiences before and after the Flood to Howard's experiences, we find that he is in a comparable position. Howard has long found the world to be a mad and corrupt place in which he takes little direct interest. In his own eyes at least, he is like the blameless Noah in that he considers himself sane while those around him are mad; and he remains sane, he believes, by simply refusing to participate in the external world, only in the well-ordered and just world of his own artistic creation. Even Frank Wirtanen, who wants to recruit Howard as a spy—in effect, to force him to participate in the madness—remarks upon Howard's pristine artistic creations: " . . . you admire pure hearts and heroes . . . you love good and hate evil . . . you believe in romance." In other words, Howard artistically projects his own preferences for a sane, ordered, and just world; and since he knows that the world as it is constituted does not share in his preferences for order, he "lives" through his creations. Even his agreement to cooperate with Wirtanen has little to do with his patriotism towards America. Instead it has to do with his being a "ham" with "an opportunity for some pretty grand acting," a man who could transfer his talents from the small stage to the greater stage of the world, still allowing "nobody [to see] the honest me I hid so deep inside."

It is only after he meets Helga that he is able to show someone the "honest me," the "me" who wants no part in the evil going on around him. And so he constructs an even grander world with his wife, a "nation of two" which, in mythic terms, takes the happy couple all the way back to the innocent nation that Adam and Eve enjoyed before the Fall, or to use the Noah story again, the little nation that Noah and his wife knew for a few shining moments on Mount Ararat before the corruption started again. In either case, he has effectively uncreated most of the world as we know it—

the greedy and politicized nations that we inhabit. Again, in both of these myths, troubles lie ahead, just as they do for Howard and the doomed Helga; but for awhile they can enjoy their own internal Eden or Mount Ararat.

Of course, the reader recognizes in Howard's contrived universe a powerful element of self-deception. To make his happy vision work, he must lie to himself. He must turn the very real madness going on outside his self-devised world into an illusion, thus paradoxically reversing, if only in his own mind, what is real and what is not. Moreover, while he is engaged in such delusive activity, he must also deny his very real role in the madness "out there." Eventually, however, the real world makes its presence felt; and Howard cannot deny its existence. Hence, after the loss of Helga, Howard's imagined world is shattered, and he becomes, he says, "a death-worshipper."

Curiously, Vonnegut is not yet ready, even at this point, to abandon the mythic imagery he has been using to describe Howard's inner existence. Instead, he constructs two other kinds of Eden which serve to underscore the failure of Howard's escapist creations. The first of these Edens takes the form of a simple reflection on life by a lonely man; the second, which is more complex, is placed within the larger context of Howard's pursuit of Genesis through love and art.

After the war, Howard spends fifteen years in New York, and he calls both the place and the time there his "purgatory," even though no real purging occurs during this time. In fact, he might well have called this harsh experience his "nation of one." Both choosing anonymity because of his status as a former Nazi and having anonymity thrust upon him by the condition of life in that mammoth place, Howard lives a simple and lonely life in an attic apartment, which he will later liken to his Berlin apartment, as we have seen. Vonnegut's point, of course, is that place in itself has no significance for Howard; and so, ironically, the physical dangers present in wartime Berlin were diminished by the happiness he made and enjoyed there and, conversely, the relative safety of a New York apartment makes for a sad and lonely existence. As Vonnegut suggests in a recent article entitled "The Lake," happiness abides in "the state of people's portable souls" and not in "immovable real estate." This concept is clearly at work in *Mother Night*. In Berlin, we are told, the happy world formed by Helga and Howard's portable souls was small indeed:

> *Das Reich der Zwei*, the nation of two my Helga and I had—its territory, the territory we defended so jealously, didn't go much beyond the bounds of our great double bed.
>
> Flat, tufted, springy little country, with my Helga and me for mountains.

This little "country" is now lost, or so he believes, though we shall see that it can be recovered again in imagination by deception.

In contrast, after the war, Howard again finds himself musing on the question of a severely limited world, only now he is excluded from that world, an outsider looking in:

> There was one pleasant thing about my ratty attic: the back window of it overlooked a little private park, *a little Eden* formed of joined back yards. That park, that Eden, was walled off from the streets by houses on all sides.
>
> It was big enough for children to play hide-and-seek in.
>
> I often heard a cry from that little Eden, a child's cry that never failed to make me stop and listen. It was the sweetly mournful cry that meant a game of hide-and-seek was over, that those still hiding were to come out of hiding, that it was time to go home.
>
> The cry was this: "Olly-olly-ox-in-free." (emphasis added)

This description is quite touching and significant, both as an indicator of Howard's yearnings and as a foreshadowing detail. Clearly he still has Edenic preoccupations, only this time he finds himself a spectator rather than a creator and an active participant in the Edenic life. Moreover, the reference to Eden here also represents a redefinition of terms. Unlike his little nation of two, this Eden takes place in the backyard world of childhood—a world where the game can be played for fun and where the game ends whenever the participants say it does. This last part appeals to Howard very much, and he does not fail to draw the conclusion that he, too, would like to inhabit a word where he can utter a familiar cry and thus "end my own endless game of hide-and-seek."

In fact, however, Howard's endless game is about to end, and, in this regard, his wish also functions to foreshadow what is to come. The change is brought about by an article in a reactionary newspaper, *The White Christian Minuteman*, which he describes as "a scabrous, illiterate, anti-Semitic, anti-Negro, anti-Catholic hate sheet." The article, which indicates Howard's whereabouts and praises his service to the Nazis during the war, has the effect of driving Howard into the open, where he becomes fair game for haters of other sorts. The Russians are using spies to get at him, and their eventual plan is to bring him to Russia, put him on trial, and use him an as example of American cooperation with the Nazis and/or America's harboring of war criminals. The Israelis also want to bring him to trial in Jerusalem, and they ultimately win out. And an American, one Bernard B. O'Hare, who captured him during the war only to see him quietly escape during the Nuremberg trials, also wants him for personal reasons. In short, though his hide-and-seek game is indeed about to end, a much more serious and heartbreaking game is about to begin.

By far the worst thing about this new game is that it involves the radical misuse of his creations, love and art, which, though he really engaged in neither during his fifteen years in New York, had nevertheless remained intellectually untainted for him. Howard has managed to believe in the integrity of his ideals, in the possibility of recreating one's own existence, even if the larger creations of history and politics are not wholly escapable. In one of his poems, Howard speaks of "the great machine of history," calling it a huge steamroller that kills, but only if one is foolish enough to stand in its path—in other words, to be an active participant in it:

> My love and I, we ran away,
> The engine did not find us.
> We ran up to a mountain top,
> Left history far behind us.
> Perhaps we should have stayed and died,
> But somehow we don't think so.
> We went to see where history'd been,
> And my, the dead did stink so.

The mountain top, presumably the Mount Ararat that he speaks of earlier, represents not their physical removal from the war (the steamroller's path), but their intellectual retreat, their refusal to give themselves over completely to the homicidal madness around them. This retreat is an internal place where, as Klinkowitz says, the self can remain inviolate. "Vonnegut's point, however," Klinkowitz goes on, "is that in this modern world the self can indeed be violated, and so is at every turn." It is this violation of self, this subversion of his mythical recreations, which ushers in the reign of Mother Night and which causes Howard in the end to prefer death to freedom.

Night's victory is accomplished not by violence (not at first at any rate) but by smooth guile and dumb luck. After thirteen years of living in seclusion in New York, Howard decides to make a small attempt to break out of his self-enclosure. With a wood-carving set bought from a military-surplus store, he carves a set of chessmen and then impulsively knocks on a neighbor's door to show him "the marvelous thing I had made," an incipient rekindling of his interest in creating things. That neighbor, as luck would have it, is himself an artist, a painter, named George Kraft. But, also as Howard's dark luck would have it, Kraft turns out to be what Howard himself once was—a spy posing as an artist—in this case, a Russian spy named Iona Potapov. Kraft also claims to be a widower who misses his wife very much, and on these bases, love and art, Howard and Kraft strike up a warm friendship. Paradoxically, despite his lies, Kraft will turn out to be both a true friend to Howard and the man responsible for Howard's undoing. For his part, Howard is so delighted with his new friend that he draws a subtle link between him and his own dead wife, Helga. Earlier in his life, after he agreed to act as an American spy, Howard decided not to tell Helga of his decision, even though, he says, it would have made no difference to her. "It would simply have made my heavenly Helga's world, which was already something to make The Book of Revelation seem pedestrian." Later, after he and Kraft become friends, he says that they "whooped it up as though Jesus had returned." These references to the Christian myth of re-creation, the time when Christ would come again to establish the New Jerusalem, are significant insofar as they are another representation of Howard's mythic yearnings. After years of loneliness, he finds in Kraft something like the mythic renewal he could achieve with Helga earlier in his life, and, for that reason, he feels reborn.

Hand in hand with the boon of finding a friend comes an even larger and more illusory blessing, this one effected by the editor of *The White Christian Minuteman*, the Reverend Doctor Lionel L. D. Jones. Jones is yet another ironic soul mate to Howard Campbell. His radical beliefs, though held throughout his life, were given widespread publication only after the death of his second wife. Prior to that time, we are told, he lived with both of his wives in "so happy, so whole, so self-sufficient a nation of two that Jones did almost nothing . . . by way of alerting the Anglo-Saxons" to the Jewish-Black-Catholic conspiracy to take over America . In other words, love is again seen here as a disarming and apolitical force, an idea that is, of course, most appealing to Howard. Moreover, the narrator also tells us that Jones's times with his first wife, during which he worked as an embalmer in a funeral home, "were golden, not only emotionally and financially, but *creatively* as well" (emphasis added). Jones's creation involved his collaboration with a chemist to make two new products: Viverine, an embalming fluid; and Gingiva-Tru, a gum-simulating substance for false teeth. In this regard, Howard regards him as a fellow artist, one who, like himself, used love and art to derive meaning in life.

The bounty that Jones brings with him when he visits Howard is nothing less than the revival of Howard's own re-creations—his love and art. Accompanying Jones is a woman who he claims is the resurrected Helga. Moreover, Helga has brought with her a trunk containing all of Howard's works, which he has assumed were lost. The emotional impact that these two rediscoveries have on Howard is strong indeed. He believes that time has take a sudden leap backwards, as evidenced by his calling the chapter in which he regains his love "The Time Machine," and that now, in middle age, he can resume the business of creating a meaningful life out of the materials that interest him, thus participating in life to the extent that he wishes while retaining his self-enclosure against the forces of chaos.

Of course, all of these boons turn out to be important elements in Howard's final undoing: Kraft, who has revealed Howard's whereabouts to Jones, has turned the privileged revelation of Howard's identity into a Russian political cause; Jones, by publishing the information, has made it possible for Howard's various "enemies" to find him; and Helga is revealed to be her sister, Resi Noth. She admits her identity after they have spent the night together at a hotel. Here is how Howard describes the morning after that happy night:

> The city was clean and hard and bright the next morning, looking like an enchanted dome that would shatter at a tap or ring like a great glass ball.
>
> My Helga and I stepped from our hotel to the sidewalk snappily. I was lavish in my courtliness, and my Helga was no less grand in her respect and gratitude. We had had a marvelous night.
>
> I was not wearing war-surplus clothing. I was wearing the clothes I had put on after fleeing from Berlin, after shucking off the uniform of the Free American Corps. . . .
>
> And all the while my Helga's small hand rested on my good left arm, creeping in an endless and erotic exploration of the tingling area between the inside of my elbow and the crest of my stringy biceps.
>
> We were on our way to buy a bed, a bed like our bed in Berlin.

They cannot buy a bed, however, because all of the shops are closed, a fact that Howard learns from a doorman at an apartment building named Sylvan House. It is, the doorman tells him, Veteran's Day, and Howard expresses annoyance over the news that the name of Armistice Day has been changed. Noting his annoyance, Helga (Resi) asks whether he hates America, to which he replies:

> "That would be as silly as loving it. . . . It's impossible for me to get emotional about it, because real estate doesn't interest me. It's no doubt a great flaw in my personality, but I can't think in terms of boundaries. . . . Virtues and vices, pleasures and pains cross boundaries at will."

Shortly thereafter, she reveals who she really is.

Vonnegut's use of allusion and imagery in this entire scene is quite provocative, functioning both to recall the invented, self-enclosed world that Howard and Helga knew and enjoyed so immensely and to prefigure the disappointment he is about to endure. Their happy night spent in erotic pleasure, their proud courtliness, his clothing, their search for a bed like the one in Berlin, which bed he earlier described as the only territory worth defending, the world as fragile, self-enclosed dome, the denial of the importance of national boundaries, Sylvan House—all of these references either directly or obliquely look backward to another time and place. By the same token, however, his self-enclosed, domed world is also all too fragile, all too vulnerable to the dark forces that he would like to shut out. With her revelation, she delivers the ring or tap that shatters the dome and the rest of his imagined happiness. In effect, she will make it possible for Night to invade the domed universe that he has created and tried to abide in.

The other subversion of Howard's invented universe concerns his art. Frank Wirtanen, Howard's Blue Fairy Godmother, reappears near the end of the novel and tells Howard not only that Kraft and Resi are Russian agents, and thus only pretending to be citizens of his nation of two or three, but also that his works have been plagiarized by one Stefan Bodovskov, a Russian who found Howard's trunk and passed the works off as his own, becoming famous and wealthy in the process. Howard's response to this news is curious. He claims to have forgotten most of his work, and so Bodovskov's theft is really not very important to him. But when Wirtanen tells him that the most famous of Bodovskov's supposed writings is a narrative called *Memoirs of a Monogamous Casanova*, an illustrated edition of which fetches forty extra rubles in Russia, Howard is profoundly disturbed. "The part of me that wanted to tell the truth," he says, "got turned into an expert liar! The lover in me got turned into a pornographer! The artist in me got turned into ugliness such as the world has rarely seen before." This violation of the personal document that represents for Howard the union of his prime creative activities—art and love—ushers in the ruinous reign of a primeval Night in his world. "*Alles kaput,*" he says of this world, and though he will return for awhile to his friends, Howard is a man who has lost what little desire to live that he might have possessed.

It seems, finally, that Vonnegut reserves the most ironic scenes in *Mother Night* for the end, for it is here, amid the crushing miscreation that his world has undergone, that Howard takes some of the most decisive steps in his life. First, he returns to his apartment and discovers, appropriately enough, that the backyard Eden outside his window is deserted, and that "there was no one in it to cry, as I should have liked someone to cry: '*Olly-*

olly-ox-in-freeeeeee.'" Yet, despite his feeling of continued bondage to the mad "game" of life, he goes on to take positive action. He begins by confronting his "own personal Fury," Bernard O'Hare, pointedly asserting his own definition of evil ("it's that large part of every man that wants to hate without limit"), assaulting O'Hare physically when he calls Howard a vile name, and finally tormenting his tormentor with the latter's own failures in life, failures that no amount of patriotic posing will undo. Following this confrontation, Howard decides to give himself up to the Israelis, though not directly. Instead, he gives himself up to a Jewish woman who lives in his apartment building, a former Auschwitzer. Ultimately, he is brought to trial in Jerusalem, and, though he is set free, again through the agency of his Blue Fairy Godmother, it is not freedom that he desires any longer; and he vows that he will hang himself that very night.

Numerous critics have commented on this final decision, most of them suggesting that Howard has finally seen fit to atone for the evil he has done. Mary Sue Schriber notes that "Campbell will not disavow responsibility for his unintended evil in the world." Likewise, Rebecca Pauly writes that "Campbell commits suicide . . . to punish himself for crimes against humanity." In an interesting comparison of Howard Campbell's confession to those of Augustine and Thomas Merton, Richard Giannone argues that, unlike the Christian writers' progress towards purgation and union with God, Howard's "guilt, punishment, and pain grope for an absolute but bring about nausea, insanity, and a desire for death." Clinton Burhans, in another provocative comparison, writes that for Vonnegut, unlike Hemingway, existence does not precede essence, and so we are not what we say we are but what we do, and "what we do at any particular time establishes the reality of what we are." According to this line of reasoning, then, Howard is guilty because he has, willingly or not, served evil in his time, both through his actions and his failures to act.

In light of Howard's attempts at mythic re-creations throughout his life, concerns that are negatively expressed in Vonnegut's very choice of a title for this novel, I would disagree with these assessments, provocative as they are. If we take at face value Howard's claim that his suicide is punishment for "crimes against *himself*" (emphasis added); and I think we should take it as such, then it follows that Howard believes not that he has caused evil in the world but that he has allowed evil to enter his own world, which is the only one that ever mattered to him. He does not take responsibility for advancing the Nazi cause or for atrocities like Auschwitz because he always considered the world mad anyway, and whatever he might have done would not have changed anything. By contrast, he tried to control his own created universe, made of art and love, and, when that fell apart, he tried to maintain the integrity through self-enclosure, through the formation of a "nation of one." By letting others violate that world after he guarded it jealously for so long, he allowed the forces of Mother Night to come in and establish her reign; and when those forces, represented by the tribunal in Jerusalem, fail to make the short work of him that he hoped they would—when, in effect, they decide to lengthen his torment in the chaotic world—he decides to take matters into his own hands.

In many ways, *Mother Night* is one of Vonnegut's most pessimistic novels because, in the end, he does not allow Howard Campbell even the solace of self-deception; and self-deception, Vonnegut suggests here and elsewhere, is a necessary ingredient in our attempt to remain sane. Indeed, it is Howard's very saneness that allows him to witness the uncreation of his world, its invasion by Chaos and Mother Night, and therein lies the horror. We should not, as some critics have, feel smug satisfaction for or see poetic justice operating in the undoing of Howard Campbell. Instead, we should feel pity for him and contempt for the kind of world that makes such conceptual re-creation necessary. We should, Vonnegut tells us, see ourselves in Howard Campbell.

JOHN L. SIMONS

Tangled Up in You:
A Playful Reading of Cat's Cradle

> . . . the two most potent
> spiritual forces in contention
> today have nothing to do with
> nations, political parties or
> economic philosophies.
>
> The opposing forces are these:
> those who enjoy childlike play-
> fulness when they become adults
> and those who don't.
> —Kurt Vonnegut

Cat's Cradle (1963) remains one of Kurt Vonnegut's least understood achievements. Sometimes the novel's complexity is underrated, as when Peter J. Reed writes, "Compared with the two preceding novels, it seems thinner in plot, more superficial and fragmentary in characterization, weaker in its ability to evoke emotions or concern, and consequently less substantial." Sometimes the novel's implications are misconstrued, as when Richard Giannone speaks of "the inquisitional cruelty of Bokononism." These problems are related, for it is necessary to grasp Vonnegut's stance

From *Critical Essays on Kurt Vonnegut*, edited by Robert Merrill. © 1990 by Robert Merrill.

toward his Bokononist materials if one is to appreciate the complexity of his fictional argument.

The crucial question is whether Vonnegut embraces the virtually nihilistic views on life expressed by a number of his characters. Vonnegut's narrator, John, originally intends to write a book about what the rest of civilization was doing on the day the first atomic bomb was dropped on Hiroshima. This book was to be entitled *The Day the World Ended*. Eventually, however, John, who is clearly his author's alter ego, chooses a different title, one that is emphatically antiapocalyptic: *Cat's Cradle*. He does so because everything in Vonnegut's fictional universe resists the impulse toward fixity, finality, or "ends" in general. As Kathryn Hume has remarked, Vonnegut sees the world as flux, involving metamorphoses, instabilities, exaggerations, and distortions. The essential "elasticity of Vonnegut's universe," Hume notes, "is just one more way of focusing attention on underlying ideas. His cosmos, consisting of endless transformations provides him with many of his literary techniques for guiding the reader's attention." What the reader is guided to see here is a fragmented world poised at the edge of chaos but potentially responsive to the far from nihilistic view of life embodied in John's and Vonnegut's title.

It is surprising how little attention has been paid to the cat's cradle as a crucial symbol in a novel of the same name. In fact Peter Reed, whose reading of *Cat's Cradle* remains the best single treatment of the book, seems to view the cat's cradle pejoratively, seeing it through the disillusioned eyes of Felix Hoenikker's midget son, Newt, as a kind of betrayal of any symbolic or meaning-making possibilities. "All incomprehensible X's. No cat. No cradle. That sums up man's dilemma as the novel shows it," writes Reed, echoing Newt's cynical observation about the string figure his father makes for him: *"No damn cat, no damn cradle."* But both critic and character have missed the point about the importance of cat's cradles in the novel. It is not the string figures themselves that Vonnegut vilifies, but rather Felix's willfully thrusting a cat's cradle at his terrified son instead of allowing the boy to play with it, in his own way, by himself.

Cat's cradles are children's playthings, but in primitive cultures they are also very popular among adults. In her book *String Figures and How to Make Them: A Study of Cat's Cradle in Many Lands*, Caroline Furness Jayne makes a number of striking observations that would seem to address the interests of a writer who received his master's degree in cultural anthropology from the University of Chicago. (Indeed, Vonnegut's thesis was *Cat's Cradle* itself.) A cat's cradle is an "endless string," that is, a cord tied together at the ends, usually about six feet long and circular. Often depicted as a symbol of infinity, it has no beginning and no end, and can be constructed into innumerable designs. Primitive cultures use cat's cradles to give shape to their own mythologies, in particular their creation tales. For example, a cat's cradle is called "Maui" in New Zealand, and as one ethnoanthropologist writes of the many string figures the natives construct, "these are said to be different scenes in their mythology, such as Hine-nui-te-po, Mother Night bringing forth her progeny, Maru and the gods, and Maui fishing up the land." *Mother Night* is, of course, the title of Vonnegut's third novel (directly preceding *Cat's Cradle*), and "Maru" recalls the foot-touching rite of "boku-maru," which is considered one of the most sacred and sensual acts of the Bokononist religion that Vonnegut invents in *Cat's Cradle*.

Foot-touching may be seen as analogous to tribesmen playing cat's cradle with each other, using two pairs of hands and often reenacting "a whole drama . . . by means of changing shapes." Groups such as the Eskimos, mentioned in *Cat's Cradle*, attach "magical" properties to their cat's cradle games, while others seem to regard them far more lightly. Vonnegut, who laments the death of magic in the modern scientific world, understands both the serious and the playful sides of cat's cradle construction. He would be charmed by the notion that ethnologists, who are after all "scientists" of culture, do not agree about the ultimate significance of string figures.

For Jayne the real interest of cat's cradles lies in "the methods employed by different races in making the figures and a comparison of those methods," not in "the study of the relations between the finished patterns." She is more concerned with the ways in which particular string figures are conceived in the minds of their makers than with the final product. How close she comes to Jerome Klinkowitz's description of the way in which Bokononism "structures" the lives of the pitiful inhabitants of Vonnegut's Caribbean island, San Lorenzo: "Here is *Cat's Cradle*'s aesthetics of belief: meaning lies not in the content of a novel or the materials of a religion, but rather in the business of dealing with them. Once that process, that act of play, is complete, content should be forgotten. If not, it becomes the stuff of great mischief." Klinkowitz follows Jayne in valuing form over content, method over pattern, process over product.

This does not mean that patterns are utterly unimportant, only that they are subject to perpetual alternation and can never be hypostasized into fixed absolutes. Nevertheless, Jayne does attempt to define three different kinds of string games that offer uncanny insights into Vonnegut's fictional creations:

1. "those figures whereof the purpose is to form final *patterns*, supposed to represent definite objects;"

2. "those which are *tricks*, wherein, after much complex manipulation of the strings, the entire loop is suddenly drawn from the hand by some simple movement; and"
3. "those which are *catches*, wherein, when certain strings are pulled, the hand or some of the figures may be unexpectedly caught in a running noose."

Jayne concludes, "Of course, there is no hard and fast rule of classification; several very pretty patterns may be converted into catches." As she implies, it is possible to combine "patterns," "tricks," and "catches" within a single cat's cradle, thus offering a sense of stability while at the same time undermining the stability, or trapping it in the web (cradle) of one's own creation. All of these allotropic elements are playfully at work in Vonnegut's own literary cat's cradle, as we see most clearly in the chapter called, appropriately, "Cat's Cradle." But before we look at that chapter we should first consider the crucial scene when little Newt Hoenikker is frightened by his father's sudden appearance bearing a string figure.

In chapter five Newt Hoenikker describes the day Dr. Felix Hoenikker plays (or so it seems) with his six-year-old son for the first and last time. By chance Dr. Hoenikker has just received the manuscript of a novel tied with mailing string. This novel was written in prison by a convicted fratricide named Marvin Sharpe Holderness. Holderness's novel concerns how "mad scientists made a terrific bomb that wiped out the whole world"; he writes to Felix Hoenikker, the inventor of the atomic bomb, because he wants to know just what to put into the bomb to make it sound authentic. Unfortunately for Marvin Holderness, Felix Hoenikker, who has never, according to his son, "read a novel or even a short story in his whole life, or at least not since he was a little boy," sets aside the manuscript and, momentarily fascinated by the loop of string he holds in his hands, "started playing with it. His fingers made the string figure called a 'cat's cradle.'" The scene is poignant because Newt, the essentially orphaned son of a living father, realizes that it was probably through a human tie, perhaps with his tailor father, that Felix learned to build cat's cradles. But Felix has long since abandoned imaginary "made-up games" for what he calls "real games," with all too real consequences for his family and for humanity. "He must have surprised himself when he made a cat's cradle out of that string," Newt continues, "and maybe it reminded him of *his own childhood*. He all of a sudden came out of his study and did something he had never done before. He tried *to play with me*. Not only had he never played with me before; he had hardly ever spoken to me" (my emphases). This towering figure, impersonal and abstract as a god, then went down on his knees, showed Newt his teeth, and waved that tangle of string in his face. "'See? See? See?' he asked. 'Cat's cradle. See the cat's cradle? See where the nice pussycat sleeps? Meow. Meow.'"

The scene appears to be harmless, even charming. But within the larger structure of the novel, and in direct relation to a particular day when nuclear Hell was unleashed on Hiroshima, it looms as darkly sinister in a book in which another kind of Hell is let loose upon the nuclear family typified by the Hoenikker children, but also the book's other physically and spiritually maimed families—the Breeds, the Mintons, the Castles, even the twice-divorced, booze-and-cigarette surfeited narrator himself.

As Felix draws nearer, Newt recoils, terrified. At a distance the father may seem a remote deity, but up close he resembles some satanic monster out of a science-fiction film. "His pores looked as big as craters on the moon," writes Newt. "His ears and nostrils were stuffed with hair. Cigar smoke made him smell like the mouth of Hell. So close up, my father was the ugliest thing I had ever seen. I dream about it all the time." Here we have what may be a gruesome parody of Joyce's description of little Stephen Dedalus, "Baby Tuckoo," gazing up at his father at the beginning of *A Portrait of the Artist as a Young Man*. Joyce's scene represents, as Hugh Kenner has written apropos of the "father with the hairy face," "a traditional infantile analogue of God the Father." But here in Vonnegut we witness the devil's almost Moloch-like appearance, his smoky rictus akin to the malodorous "mouth of Hell." The reference may be more deeply Dantean than we initially suspect. Considering that Felix Hoenikker is a form of anti-Christ, inflicting on man both nuclear war and perpetual winter, his actions as a scientist echo the words of Dante's Charon, ferryman to the underworld, who tells Dante and Virgil that he comes to lead them "into eternal dark, into fire and ice." The journey through the Inferno parallels Felix Hoenikker's inventions of the atomic bomb and *ice-nine*. In the initial stages of Dante's descent Hell's circles are generally hot, but when Dante arrives in the last circle, the ninth, he finds instead a "huge frozen lake," filled with those sinners whose sins involved "denials of love and of all human warmth," which is another way of defining Felix Hoenikker's relationship to his late wife, his children, and people in general.

At the very center of Dante's final circle of Hell, immobilized and up to his neck in ice, is Satan, perpetrator of the most destructive of all impulses, nihilism. In this vein he resembles the more comic but no less nihilistic Felix Hoenikker. Seemingly childlike and often referred to as "innocent," Felix nevertheless wreaks the same kind of doomsday havoc as Satan. In fact Vonnegut makes one of his strongest anti-nihilistic statements by pairing a would-be artist named Krebbs, who destroys John's apartment, with

Hoenikker himself. As his final act of devastation Krebbs kills a cat by hanging it on the refrigerator door handle and placing under it a sign written in excrement that reads "Meow." This, of course, is no cradle but a cat's gallows, and Krebbs, like Hoenikker, is a man who really believes in nothing. Krebbs destroys a cat, Felix Hoenikker a cat's cradle (symbol of imagination). Felix's insistent "Meow, Meow" is really no less nihilistic than Krebbs's sign. Neither science nor art can function without some respect for humanity, as both Felix (whose first name ironically evokes a famous cartoon cat) and Krebbs illustrate.

Felix Hoenikker's nihilistic egotism is fully in evidence in the scene with the cat's cradle. The father puts a tangled mass of string before his cowering child, who sees through it into Felix's horrific face. The father then proceeds to hold up *his* version of a cat's cradle and to sing *his* version of the nursery rhyme lullaby "Rockaby Baby," where a baby's cradle or human arms as a cradle figure so importantly. In the conceit of the cat's cradle metamorphosing into the baby cradle, Newt becomes the cat (or baby) falling when the wind blows, but with no one there to catch him. No wonder the boy "burst into tears" and "jumped up and ran out of the house as fast as I could go." For Newt, no cat's cradle means no "catch" and no catcher for the falling boy. The image is Salingeresque, the experience a nightmare; when he "grows up," Newt continues to paint that traumatic nightmare in the form of black "blasted landscapes," post-nuclear in their evocation of a ruined world. Newt's cynical *"No damn cat! No damn cradle"* underscores his sense, screened and deflected of course, of his own personal damnation before his father's indifference.

Any knowledgeable student of child psychology or of play therapy knows that Felix Hoenikker is not really *playing* with his son because it is he and not Newt who is manipulating the string figure. Devoid of a proper "mother," whom Alice Miller defines as "the person closest to the child during the first years of life," someone who can properly "mirror" the child's emerging identity and allow that child to grow *as a self*, Newt can only blame the cat's cradle for holding no cat and being no cradle. In essence he negates his own imagination, though the real cause of this crippling loss is not the string figure but his father, the absent "mother," the missing cradle rocker. What Newt fails to understand is that cat's cradles are not meant to be "real" in a scientific or factual sense. Rather they are games for us to play with and to act upon. They are useful fictions. Without them we cannot "invent" our own lives, are doomed to repeat endlessly (as Newt does with his paintings) our moment of loss.

What does "play" accomplish for a child, and why is its absence felt so profoundly? As defined by Bruno Bettelheim, play "refers to the young child's activities characterized by freedom from all but personally imposed rules (which are changed at will), by free-wheeling fantasy involvement, and by absence of any goals outside the activity itself." Remove play and games from a child and he or she loses the "chance to work through unresolved problems of the past, to deal with pressures of the moment, and to experiment with various roles and forms of social interaction in order to determine their suitability for himself." Bettelheim emphasizes that *real play* (a delicious Bokononist paradox) is "a child's true reality; this takes it far beyond the boundaries of its meaning for adults." Without play a child is shaped, formed, carved—like a statue—by the adult world. With play the child develops an "inner life," a fluid self that nevertheless begins to explore, to experiment "with moral identities." Games like "cops and robbers" are salutary, even if they deal in mimed violence, because "such conflicts between good and evil represent the battle between tendencies of the asocial id and those of the diametrically opposed superego," and they permit as well "some discharge of aggression either actually or symbolically, through conflict." Once again "play" sounds acutely Bokononist in its acting out of both sides of a moral struggle. And while Bettelheim seems to identify the formation of an ego with the forces of the superego gaining "ascendancy to control or overbalance those of the id," both Bettelheim and Vonnegut are conscious of the need to play in order to become a self. Nor would Bettelheim dispute Bokonon's exhortation to his followers to become "actors in a play they understood, that any human being anywhere could understand." Little wonder then that Bokonon describes growing up as "a bitter disappointment for which no remedy exists, unless laughter can be said to remedy anything." It is a tragedy for an adult to lose the ability to play, but unlike a child, and unlike the infantile, narcissistic Felix Hoenikker as well, the adult who plays can only be a good Bokononist if he realizes that he *is* playing, that his actions may have negative consequences (the A-bomb, *ice-nine*), and that if this is so they should be abandoned. That is what Vonnegut means by the epigraph to *Cat's Cradle*, where he instructs his audience to "Live by the foma ("Harmless untruths") that make you brave and kind and healthy and happy." The key word here is "Harmless."

A discussion of play is important to art because creativity is an aspect of play and functions only when the artist-self exists in what D. W. Winnicott calls an "unintegrated state of personality," a condition in which the artist is able to act upon the "formless experience" of his or her life and to play with it, make something mysterious, flexible, and free out of it. Like Bettelheim and Vonnegut, Winnicott believes that without play the child's growth process is stunted and self-making cannot take place. As Winnicott writes, "To get to the idea of playing it is helpful to think of the *preoccupations* that characterize the playing of a young child. *The content does not matter.* What matters is the near-withdrawal state. . . . " (first emphasis Winnicott's, second emphasis mine). Play is one of the "transitional phenomena" that Winnicott has explored so extensively in his work. It inhabits a mediating middle ground between the empirical and the invented worlds: "This area of playing is not inner psychic reality. It is outside the individual, but it is not the external world." Once again play is very Bokononist because, while Bokononism refuses to blink at the hard truth of a reality it cannot alter, it nevertheless fictionalizes that reality. Bokonon's principle of "Dynamic Tension," which derives from Charles Atlas and has appeared in children's comic books for years, closely follows the double vision (internal and external) of play. "Dynamic Tension" also resembles the making of string figures: "It is the same principle whereby if you hold your hands apart, pulling in opposite directions, you can string a cat's cradle on them; with no tension, of course, you would just have a muddle of string." Just as Bokononism is tough work for its followers, a point that few critics seem to note, play is tough work for its earnest youthful adherents. This is so because in play a child attempts to give constructive form to the world's fundamental disorder. That is what makes it, in Winnicott's words, "inherently exciting and precarious."

It is no happenstance that Winnicott himself employed string therapy games, analogous offshoots of cat's cradles, in treating disturbed children. And it is no chance occurrence that in one of those string games a boy named Edmund took a mound of tangled string, placed it "at the bottom of [a] bucket like bedding, and began to put [his] toys in, so that they had a nice soft place to lie in, like a cradle or a cot." Or a cat's cradle. What Edmund learns, and what both Bettelheim and Winnicott have taught us, is the vital necessity of play in the development of a child's psychic life. Without it we have the blighted freakish children of Felix Hoenikker, father of the atomic bomb, father of *ice-nine*, but failed father to his own children. This leads us, finally, to the most important section of *Cat's Cradle*.

In the chapter called "Cat's Cradle" Newt describes one of his scratchy morbid paintings as the depiction of a cat's cradle. John asks if the scratches are string. Newt responds, "One of the oldest games there is, cat's cradle. Even the Eskimos know it! . . . For maybe a hundred thousand years or more, grownups have been waving tangles of string in their children's faces." John's only response is "Um," but Newt proceeds, obviously anxious to make his point. He holds out his black painty hands (a gesture John himself unconsciously imitates throughout the novel) as though a cat's cradle were strung between them: "No wonder kids grow up crazy. A cat's cradle is nothing but a bunch of X's between somebody's hands, and the little kids look and look and look at all those X's." "And?" John asks. Newt replies, *"No damn cat, and no damn cradle."* For Newt, then, cat's cradles represent lies, betrayals, perfidy, the end of imagination rather than the beginning. "X" equals nothing, and all possibility for creation is denied. It is a nihilistic image and functions in direct relation to other forms of closure or death in the novel, specifically the dropping of the atomic bomb and the end of the world through *ice-nine*.

Everything about Vonnegut's fictional world rebukes closure and confutes endings, apocalyptic or otherwise. Thus Vonnegut begins to deconstruct Newt's pointed observations at the same moment Newt makes them. Vonnegut does so initially through a description of the fantastic house built by Mona Aamons Monzano's father, Nestor, one of the few good fathers in any of Vonnegut's novels. Understanding this house is vital to understanding how the cat's cradle figure (itself architectural) dominates this chapter. The house resembles in part Coleridge's stately pleasure dome, for it is clearly a Bokononist home, grounded in physical reality but transcending that reality at the same time. Built on the side of the putatively mythic Mount McCabe, highest point on the island of San Lorenzo, and rising through ethereal mists, the house is formed out of "a cunning lattice of very light steel posts and beams," with interstices "variously open, chinked with native stone, glazed or curtained by sheets of canvas." Such terms as "cunning lattice," "variously open," "curtained," and "canvas" seem deliberately to evoke the structure's clever design, its freedom (openness), its artfulness (curtain and canvas allude to both drama and painting), as well as to cat's cradles themselves (the criss-crossed lattice), and are all used to undercut Newt's debunking of string figures. Of Nester Aamons John writes, "The effect of the house was not so much to enclose as to announce that a man had been whimsically busy there." Like the house, Vonnegut's fiction defies definition, shows a man "Busy, busy, busy," or what "we Bokononists say when we feel that a lot of mysterious things are going on." The real mystery, sourceless, inexplicable, and "measureless to man," as Coleridge would put it, is the mystery of creation or play, the magic of cat's cradles themselves, fragile and fantastic forms, stretched delicately over an abyss (here the mountainside), yet infinitely free.

Asleep in a butterfly chair on that improbably poised "giddy terrace," itself "framed in a misty view of sky, sea, and valley," making it a part of nature and yet different from it, Newt dreams his grim dreams, then wakes to describe for John his spooky, grotesque paintings. And they *are* repellent, "small and black and warty," consisting of "scratches made in a black, gummy impasto." "The scratches formed a sort of spider's web," continues John, "and I wondered if they might not be the sticky nets of human futility hung upon a moonless night to dry." Here is the opposite image of a cat's cradle, which liberates the mind, for this cradle is a sticky "spider's web," image of human futility, that which entraps us in our own natures and finally kills us. There can be little doubt that Vonnegut himself identifies in part with this vision. But only in part. This is a vision halved, unfinished, all darkness without light, evil without good, despair without hope. It is, in short, an anti-Bokononist perception of the world, the specter of a fallen cradle, a blighted childhood (like Newt's), lacking the "Dynamic Tension" that precariously balances its paradoxical oppositions so that human life is possible despite our pathetic condition.

Appropriately Newt, whose dreams are violent, wakes to the sound of gunfire, an explosion not unlike a bomb blast, that propels him into the previously cited "reading" of his own painting. But there is little difference between Newt and what he paints. Here is Newt putting "his black, painty hands to his mouth and chin, leaving black smears there. He rubbed his eyes and made black smears around them too." His painting may be "something different" to others who see it, as a work of art should be, but to Newt it is one thing only, the objectification of his father's betrayal of Newt's childhood, symbolized by the destruction of a cat's cradle. In an important sense Newt has not yet been born because he has not been allowed to experience his childhood. We see the little man "curled" prenatally (perhaps even like a cat!) in that big butterfly chair, still waiting to metamorphose, to fly himself.

Everything that surrounds Newt and John on that wondrous terrace seems to symbolize the fertile life-affirming impulse. The mountain, whale-shaped and hump-like at the top, may also have connotations relating it to Mona Aamons Monzano, the would-be earth goddess with whom John is in love and whom he marries. Surely Vonnegut intends the pun on "a mons," as in "mons veneris." But if the mountain represents in part female fertility, then the stream and waterfall that flow down its side imply the opposite or male potential for life. These two forces, male and female, unite in Nestor Aamon's house, which, in a sexually charged image, "straddled a waterfall." In addition the mountain and the waterfall share the Bokononist oppositions of fixity and flow, what might be called the novel's flexible form, its ceaseless mediation between chaos and order.

Having suffered at birth the loss of his natural mother, little Newt cannot comprehend the abundant powers that nature itself figures forth around him. Nor can he see how Nestor Aamons's own design unites the natural with the human-made, the artful creation out of what is already there. Vonnegut makes this apparent in an outrageous pun that underscores the union between art and life in *Cat's Cradle*. The pun turns on a parody of

Stanley's search for the lost explorer Livingstone through the "heart" of darkest Africa. In the novel a plump servant—rare in poverty-ridden San Lorenzo—guides John to his room, a journey "around the heart of the house, down a staircase of *living stone*, a staircase sheltered or exposed by steel-framed rectangles at random. My bed was a foam-rubber slab on a stone shelf, a shelf of *living stone*. The walls of my chamber were canvas. Stanley demonstrated how I might roll them up or down, as I pleased" (my emphases). Led by the servant Stanley, John journeys into the "heart" of Nestor Aamons's house to a bedroom hard by the "living stone" of the mountainside, stone that contains an even more female image of a cave beneath the waterfall, festooned with what resemble ancient prehistoric drawings but which, in contradistinction to Newt's morbid modernistic paintings, are primitive drawings that "treated endlessly the aspects of Mona Aamons Monzano as a little girl." These apparently ancient but actually quite recent playful paintings refute Newt's limited vision and make an indirect comment on his never having been born out of the womb of creation, while the sensual earth mother, Mona, revels in her own fertility / creativity.

Vonnegut offers one final negative verdict on little Newt's vision of art and life through the saintly yet sinister figure of Julian Castle, famous Schweitzer-like doctor at the House of Hope and Mercy. It is Castle whom John originally intended to visit on his journey to San Lorenzo, and it is Castle who gives the final verdict on Newt's jaundiced artistic vision. Castle, who has witnessed and attempted to give comfort to the worst kinds of human misery, including bubonic plague, gazes upon Newt's canvas and says, "It's *black*. What is it—hell?" Receiving no help from Newt, Castle snarls, in his best Edward G. Robinson voice, "Then it's hell." From someone who has seen the hell of human suffering on his god-forsaken island, this seems to ring true. But Castle is a true Bokononist and really means the opposite of what he says. Therefore when he learns from John that the painting is of a cat's cradle, he replies that it is in fact "a picture of the meaninglessness of it all! I couldn't agree more." Castle is really mocking Newt's cynical attitudinizing, pushing Newt into either agreeing with him or abandoning his pose. "You may quote me," Castle continues. "Man is vile, and man makes nothing worth making, knows nothing worth knowing!" At this point, after winning Newt's uneasy assent (Newt seems "to suspect momentarily that the case had been a little overstated"), Castle picks up the "blasted landscape" of a painting and hurls it off the cantilevered terrace, from which it boomerangs and slices into the waterfall.

The painting flows into the maelstrom of the waterfall and down the mountainside, where it "ends" (or seems to) in a "big stone bowl," across which the poor natives have woven out of chicken wire a net (a cat's cradle?) that they use to catch and hold whatever flows down from above. Here is what they find: "Four square feet of gummy canvas, the four milled and mitred sticks of the stretcher, some tacks, too, and a cigar. All in all, a pretty nice *catch* for some poor, poor man" (my emphasis). The proper "use" to which Newt's limited and limiting "artwork" has been put belies its maker's original intention. As we have seen, a "catch" is also a kind of cat's cradle. This time it is used not only to catch Newt's painting, but figuratively to "catch" Newt himself in an unbokononist lie.

Although *Cat's Cradle* concludes with another of Newt's cynical refrains, this time in criticism of his sister Angela's loveless marriage, Newt once again sees only part of the picture. His gloss on Angela's deluded love for her ruthless husband, "See the cat? See the cradle?," can hardly be gainsaid. But the way in which, out of *her* art, Angela translates her suffering into the cadenzaed grief and grandeur of her music leads to transcendence of that miserable marriage. This cannot be said of Newt.

At the end of the book, when John searches for a "magnificent symbol" to carry with him to the top of Mount McCabe to give a central meaning to his life (he still is a Christian, and to a Christian such "centers" are important), John can find nothing, least of all a cat's cradle, to take with him. By this time *ice-nine* has nearly destroyed the world, leaving only a small enclave of survivors, among them John and Newt, still alive on San Lorenzo. What could one possibly bring to the top of a supposedly holy mountain, and what use would it be? We already know what Bokonon thinks of such gestures. As Frank Hoenikker tells John, Mount McCabe may have once been "sacred or something," but no more. John then asks, "What *is* sacred to Bonkononists?" and receives the terse reply, "Man. That's all. Just man!" Nevertheless, John continues to seek the proper symbol to carry to the top of the mountain and, one might argue, to "end" the novel on which he has been working for the past six months. He does not find that symbol by undergoing a conventional quest. Instead, unwittingly, he enacts a Bokononist "solution"—open-ended, inconclusive, ambiguous, and decentered—to his search. He discovers, whether he knows it or not, a cat's cradle.

Driving across San Lorenzo, John proffers his scheme to Newt, who by this time has become somewhat of a Bokononist. "I took my hands from the wheel for an instant to show him how empty of symbols they were. 'But what in hell would the right symbol *be*, Newt? What in hell would it *be*?' I grabbed the wheel again." Then a little later: "'But what, for the love of God, is supposed to be in my hands?'" Holding up his empty hands, as if to pantomime the making of a cat's cradle, John, a writer for whom that cat's cradle functions as a metaphor for writing, can only put them down in defeat.

Still, he is beginning to speak the paradoxical language of a Bokononist. His parallel but thematically contrasting phrases, "What in hell" and "what, for the love of God," seem to fit perfectly with the Bokononist counterpointing of those two "separate" forces of good and evil, heaven and hell, which are a part of the Bokononist mythology. In addition, that same phrase, "for the love of God," echoes an earlier exhortation on the part of Julian Castle to his son and John, both writers, not to abandon their craft just because it all seems so hopeless: "for the love of god, both of you, please keep writing!" We remember as well that it is Julian Castle who offers a capsule definition of the very writing style, cat's cradlelike, that Vonnegut invents for his novel. That something "sacred" John hopes to carry to the top of the mountain affiliates writing with responsibility as Julian Castle imagines it, for to write is to create books that entail "a *sacred* obligation to produce beauty and enlightenment and comfort at top speed" (my emphasis).

John also believes that one of his chief purposes in climbing Mount McCabe is to discover the identity of his *karass*. "If you find your life *tangled* up with somebody else's life for no very logical reasons," writes Bokonon, "that person may be a member of your *karass*." John learns that the "tendrils" of his life "began to *tangle* with those of [the Hoenikker] children" (my emphases). Vital to understanding how a *karass* works is to view it as a creation of God, not man. Thus we can never know for certain who is part of our *karass*, and it is difficult to exclude anyone from it. One thing we do know is that "a 'karass' ignores national, institutional, occupational, familial, and class boundaries." A *karass* is, finally, "as free-form as an amoeba" —or a cat's cradle. It is those words "tangled" and "tangle," associated throughout the novel with cat's cradles (beginning with Felix Hoenikker's waving a "tangled mass of string" before his cowering son, and culminating with Newt's own tangled splotchy paintings of cat's cradles), that imply a connection with the flexible, playful structures called cat's cradles, which we make and unmake, tangle and untangle, never arriving at any final synthesis of their polymorphous possibilities, never knowing what the Platonic essence of a cat's cradle could possibly be. The same is true of our *karass*, for if it is a successful *karass* we never learn who belongs to it and who does not. It is analogous to the Christian notion of grace, of being chosen for eternal salvation out of God's mysterious and ineffable love. It should make us more loving, more "human," for Bokonon worships the human above all other values.

The final chapter of *Cat's Cradle*, entitled "The End," may represent the end of *The Books of Bokonon*, of John's book, and of Vonnegut's book as well (not to mention the end of the world), but it is not a true ending. It can be no more than a cat's cradle, circular, supple, full of possibilities. If each of the many chapters in *Cat's Cradle* is a mini-cat's cradle itself, open to innumerable interpretations, then what is its ending but a beginning? By allowing Bokonon, wise but perdurably mendacious (as in the sense of "foma"), to utter the novel's final words, Vonnegut suggests that those words are suspect. Bokonon in fact duplicates John's own desperate gesture and in so doing gives it the lie. Here is the last "book" in *The Books of Bokonon:*

> If I were a younger man, I would write a history of human stupidity; and I would climb to the top of Mount McCabe and lie down on my back with my history for a pillow; and I would take from the ground some of the blue-white poison that makes statues of men; and I would make a statue of myself, lying on my back, grinning horribly, and thumbing my nose at You Know Who.

Those words are not really addressed so much to the plight of the crazy old Bokonon as to the "young man," John, to whom Bokonon speaks. In the fabulist hyper-fictional world of *Cat's Cradle*, Bokonon, the first half of whose name is an obvious respelling of the word "book," is really the author's creation. We recall that Bokonon's "real" name is Johnson, that Johnson, alias Bokonon, is really "John's son," his author's imagined progeny, and that each of them is Von's son since Johnson became the maker of *The Books of Bokonon* the year he landed on the fictional (but all too real) island of San Lorenzo, which was 1922, the year Kurt Vonnegut was born. Wheels within wheels, and cat's cradles generating newer and more elaborately concatenated cat's cradles in the perpetual process of creation, without beginning and without end.

   That is the true meaning of Vonnegut's book, and that is why, despite the imminent demise of the world and of Bokonon himself (now that his creator has become a Bokononist, as he tells us in the novel's first pages, Bokonon's existence is no longer necessary; he has been assimilated into John), suicide is the least Bokononist solution to the desperate situation we witness at the end of *Cat's Cradle*. This, plus the realization that Bokonon is always lying, should prevent us from assuming that John intends to follow Bokonon's advice (an anti-Bokononist response). Indeed, John assumes Bokonon's conditional phrase, "If I were a younger man," into his own writing, takes the last page of *The Books of Bokonon*, and, by changing that conditional "If" to an emphatic "When," incorporates them into the beginning of his own book. John is really satirizing his own pre-Bokononist youth, its failures and its futility, when he writes, "When I was a younger man—two wives ago, 250,000 cigarettes ago, 3,000 quarts of booze ago . . . When I was a much younger man, I began to collect material for a book to be called *The Day the World Ended*." But the world does not quite end in *Cat's Cradle*, and its author, holding in his hands the only cat's cradle he knows, that is his fictional world, can hardly take the advice of Bokonon and thumb his nose at "You Know Who," since he does not in fact know who "You Know Who" is, or whether "He" even exists. Bokononism is referred to as a religion in *Cat's Cradle*, but if it is it is a very different, undogmatic religion, built out of the creative, playful, childlike aspects of human nature, out of our enduring ability to invent meanings in an essentially meaningless world (or a world whose meanings are hidden permanently from us). By *not* following Bokonon's advice, John enacts his own conversion to Bokononism.

Bokononism is a philosophy of flow, resisting entropy and harrowing the fixities that reduce societies to monomaniacal obsessions, to one-sided "truths." Everything it stands for opposes the destructive science of Felix Hoenikker, and for that reason it is fiercely if amusingly unquietistic, refusing to accept that all human action is ultimately futile. Thus it is stridently unlike another Vonnegutian "philosophy" with which it is often paired, the deterministic Tralfamadorianism of *Slaughterhouse-Five*. Because they hold that we are powerless to alter history (in fact "history" has already happened, and the universe has already been destroyed), Vonnegut's Tralfamadorians believe that our only solution is to time-travel, to live in selected "happy moments," to ignore the burden of human misery that drives Bokonon mad but which also forces him to invent a religion of compassion and compensation against our grim human lot. Contrastingly, the Tralfamadorians see humankind in the lowliest terms, as "bugs trapped in amber" for whom they have little sympathy.

Although their reductivist philosophy appeals to such a pathetic and limited person as Billy Pilgrim, the protagonist of *Slaughterhouse-Five*, it is difficult to believe that Vonnegut wants us all to become Tralfamadorians. Bokononism, on the other hand, is Dostoevskian in its riddling contradictions. A true Tralfamadorian would never accept Bokononism's life-lie, its "cruel paradox," which acknowledges "the heartbreaking necessity of lying about reality, and the heartbreaking impossibility of lying about it." For "heartbreaking" read "tragic," a word utterly alien to Tralfamadorian hedonism. So much deeper and more complicated than Tralfamadorianism, Bokononism is at bottom a comic response to a tragic world, yet a response that simultaneously *contains*, in its artful dualism (really a delicate balancing), both the tragic and the comic aspects of human nature.

There is no better gloss on Bokononism than the celebrated description of the artistic imagination offered by F. Scott Fitzgerald in *The Crack-Up*. "[L]et me," writes Fitzgerald, "make a general observation—the test of a first-rate intelligence is the ability to hold two opposed ideas in the mind at the same time, and still retain the ability to function." What follows is critical if we are to comprehend Vonnegut's tragicomic Bokononist vision. "One should, for example," Fitzgerald continues, "be able to see that things are hopeless and yet be determined to make them otherwise." Kurt Vonnegut could easily have penned these words. What's more, Vonnegut's own rhetoric follows Fitzgerald's in the latter's summation of his hope-against-hope philosophy: "I must hold in balance the sense of the futility of effort and the sense of the necessity to struggle: the conviction of the inevitability of failure and still the determination to succeed." This is, of course, the language of Vonnegut's "cruel paradox." It is the voice of tragedy, which for Vonnegut, confirmed Bokononist that he is, can only be expressed by its opposite, the author's courageous comedy.

LEONARD MUSTAZZA

Divine Folly and the Miracle of Money in
God Bless You, Mr. Rosewater

At one point in *God Bless You, Mr. Rosewater*, a lawyer who represents the
financial interests of an idealistic young man tries to set the latter straight
about the ways of the world. Claiming that one of the principal tasks of his
law firm is "the prevention of saintliness on the part of our clients," the older
man delivers this piece of practical wisdom to his misguided young client:

> "Every year at least one young man whose affairs we manage
> comes into our office, wants to give his money away. He has
> completed his first year at some great university. It has been an
> eventful year! He has learned of unbelievable suffering around
> the world. He has learned of the great crimes that are at the
> roots of so many family fortunes. He has had his Christian nose
> rubbed, often for the very first time, in the Sermon on the
> Mount. . . . [W]hen I see the effect [such an education] has on
> certain young people, I ask myself, 'How dare a university
> teach compassion without teaching history, too?' History tells
> us this . . . if it tells us nothing else: Giving away a fortune is a
> futile and destructive thing. . . . Cling to your miracle. . . .
> Money is dehydrated Utopia. This is a dog's life for almost

From *Forever Pursuing Genesis: The Myth of Eden in the Novels of Kurt Vonnegut* by Leonard
Mustazza. © 1990 by Associated University Presses, Inc.

49

everybody. . . . But, because of your miracle, life for you and
yours can be a paradise!"

This statement, made by a minor character and placed unobtrusively enough
late in the novel, well describes the philosophical tensions that Vonnegut
deals with in his fifth novel, which many critics have called his best to that
point. One of the leading characters in this book, the narrator tells us at the
outset, is a sum of money; and as a character, it will function as both
protagonist and antagonist, as representative of lifesaving humility and life-
denying pride, as myth-based symbol of the good and the ugly in human
history. Indeed, the story is perhaps less about people than it is about
attitudes toward money—attitudes that are reflected in two kinds of myth,
both of them announced in the lawyer's quote above: the myth of the
American utopia, based as it is on material advancement (hence, money as
"miracle," as "dehydrated Utopia," as maker of paradise); and Christian
views of money, inhumanity, and damnation as projected in one of the
principal New Testament myths, the Sermon on the Mount.

In keeping with the thesis of this study, I would like to focus on Eliot
Rosewater as the heir to one of these myths and the proponent of the other.
Like Paul Proteus, Malachi Constant, Winston Niles Rumfoord, Howard
Campbell, and like the "powers" of San Lorenzo, Eliot pursues Genesis,
both literally and figuratively. He tries to remake his world in accordance
with a model that appeals to him. Unlike most of his counterparts in
Vonnegut's earlier works, however, he is far less concerned with his own
good than that of others, whoever they may be. Having money and,
therefore, power, Eliot takes upon himself the role of god-player; but, unlike
Rumfoord, who does essentially the same thing, this fabulously rich
American wants to reverse the dominant ideas about power held by the
powerful. For Eliot, kindness is an art form. Yet, unlike Howard Campbell,
he does not want to recreate only his own life but those of discarded, useless,
and unattractive Americans. Through his "art," he hopes to redeem such
people, and to reaffirm, in Leonard Leff's words, "the magnetic chain of
humanity—the relationship of one man to another." Jerome Klinkowitz has
quite correctly suggested that Vonnegut, here and in his other novels, refuses
to accept the world at face value. Rather, he "chooses to show just how
arbitrary and conventional the 'world' is, and how easily it may be changed
for something better." Though such change is at the heart of every Vonnegut
novel, *Rosewater* (and again nearly a decade and a half later, *Jailbird*)
specifically, albeit ironically, depicts the effects of massive social action, of
"folly" that, flying as it does in the face of conventional wisdom, represents
the best hope we have for anything like real justice, and of an alternative,

inner-directed American utopia that reconciles the competing myths of material prosperity and Christian compassion.

A few critics have noticed in passing the connection that Vonnegut draws between these competing myths. In his review essay, Leslie Fiedler asserts that "we remember the novel chiefly as a book about madness, or more particularly, one about the relationship between madness and holiness," and, in this regard, he goes on to say that Kilgore Trout, the science-fiction writer whom Eliot admires so much, plays "an equivocal St. Paul to Eliot Rosewater's absurd Christ." Citing Vonnegut's references to both the Old and the New Testament, Max Schultz argues that the novel contrasts an earlier vision of America as the new Eden and the "junk yard" it has become. Into this junkyard, he goes on, comes Eliot Rosewater, prepared to offer money and love to the poor in body and spirit. Yet the question of Eliot's sanity prompts Schultz to doubt the novel's moral stance. "Even the title is a stand-off," he writes, "with the first half . . . reminding us of Christ's teachings on love, and the second half ('Or Pearls Before Swine'") reiterating the Sermon on the Mount's warning against wasting the gift of the Kingdom of Heaven on those who will not enter it." And Richard Giannone sees Eliot not as a divine figure himself, but rather as a kind of prophet: "Love is Eliot's new god to repair the blasphemed life, the exploitation, brought through worship of Mammon." As such, Giannone suggests that Eliot's activities on behalf of the poor should be regarded "not as mere philanthropy but as sacred to the core." There are a few other such arguments about the biblical and literary allusions that Vonnegut employs in his characterization of this eccentric man, but those cited above show the general tenor of the critical appraisals.

Of course, all of these arguments are valid enough. I think, however, that it would be more revealing for my purposes here to consider the divisions of Genesis, that Vonnegut gives us: one of those divisions, reflecting an older and, for Eliot's purposes, outdated model, corresponds to the spirit of the Old Testament; the other, suggesting newer ways of looking at human relations, is consonant with the supplementary moral laws projected in such texts as the Sermon on the Mount and the Pauline epistles. To be sure, however, the division of these ideas is not nearly so tidy as this bald assertion indicates. Vonnegut is never that obvious. Instead, as we shall see, the mythic implications in the novel are, in effect, circular, moving from old law to new and then back to beginnings or Genesis.

In the manner of many biblical narratives, *Rosewater* begins with what appears to be a formal genealogy, placed in a letter from Eliot to whoever succeeds him as heir to the vast Rosewater fortune. Biblical genealogies are used for two essential purposes: to advance a narrative or to establish prestigious descent. The first of these is seen in the record of Adam's descendants, which moves the story rapidly forward from the banishment of Cain to the selection of Noah as God's instrument of re-creation—a progression that takes up a mere chapter (Genesis 5) but that involves some nine generations over thousands of years, since biblical life spans are said to take up eight or nine centuries. The other use of biblical genealogy is evident in the record of Christ's ancestors at the beginning of Matthew's gospel, where the evangelist, a rabbi, is concerned with establishing Christ's royal lineage dating back to King David. Interestingly, Vonnegut weaves both of these biblical uses into Eliot's genealogical discussion, which functions both to diminish conventional ways of thinking about prestigious ancestry and to establish Eliot's attitudes and, more generally, the theme of the novel itself.

The Rosewater dynasty was begun by a man named for the biblical dynastic figure responsible for reestablishment of humanity after the Flood. Noah Rosewater, Eliot's great-grandfather, was "a humorless, constipated Christian farm boy turned speculator and briber during and after the Civil War"; a man who, rather than marching idealistically off to war like his brother, profited from the war by his realization that "no amount of money was too much to pay for the restoration of the Union"; a man whose motto might well have been, according to Eliot, "Grab too much, or you'll get nothing at all." Self-consciously imitating biblical style, Eliot goes on: "And Noah begat Samuel," another unscrupulous and acquisitive Rosewater, whose motto was even more harsh and arrogant than his father's: "Anybody who thought that the United States of America was supposed to be a Utopia was a piggy, lazy, God-damned fool." In addition to inheriting his father's business enterprises, Samuel also bought up newspapers, thus leading the family toward more prestigious intellectual achievement. In keeping with this progression, "Samuel begat Lister Ames Rosewater," Eliot's father, whose by now old money allows him to forego business altogether and to pursue a genteel life in politics as senator from Indiana. This genealogy, of course, concludes with Eliot himself, who, he asserts without much self-pity, "begat . . . not a soul," who, unlike his greedy and pretentious forefathers, "became a drunkard, a Utopian dreamer, a tinhorn saint, an aimless fool." Given the details Eliot chooses to provide about his forebears, this line of descent, though echoing biblical language, is actually quite ironic. Contrary to Matthew's intent in providing a distinguished background for Jesus, or for that matter the intent of anyone desiring to boast of his or her long and august pedigree, Eliot's purpose here is to show the moral warts of his ancestors, to demonstrate that their fortune was ill-earned and arrogantly tended, to suggest the bogus foundation of many wealthy people's pretensions to inherited gentility, and to mock himself.

By the same token, however, Eliot's revelation of his own attitudes toward his forebears subtly carries out the other function of biblical genealogy—the advancement of the story line. Eliot's point in this epistle is not merely to inform his unknown successor about the family whose fortune he or she now controls; but to instill in that person his own attitudes about wealth, distinguished pedigree, and the American utopia, and to recommend the spirit in which he would like to see the Rosewater fortune used. He does these things by openly criticizing not only his forebears but the very nation that produced them:

> When the United States of America, which was meant to be a Utopia for all, was less than a century old, Noah Rosewater and a few men like him demonstrated the folly of the Founding Fathers in one respect: those sadly recent ancestors had not made it the law of the Utopia that the wealth of each citizen should be limited. This oversight was engendered by a weak-kneed sympathy for those who loved expensive things, and by the feeling that the continent was so vast and valuable, and the population so thin and enterprising, that no thief, no matter how fast he stole, could more than mildly inconvenience anyone. . . .
>
> Thus did a handful of rapacious citizens come to control all that was worth controlling in America. Thus was the savage and stupid and entirely inappropriate . . . American class system created. . . .
>
> *E pluribus unum* is surely an ironic motto to inscribe on the currency of this Utopia gone bust, for every grotesquely rich American represents property, privileges, and pleasures that have been denied the many.

Eliot ends his genealogical diatribe with some heartfelt advice: "Be generous. Be kind. . . . Be a sincere, attentive friend to the poor." In this way, Eliot has established the polarities between which the novel will operate, with the proud rich and those who aspire to be vying for supremacy against this "Utopian dreamer," one who still sees the possibility of remaking the American spirit.

Of course, Eliot does more than just preach. He also lives his own life in accordance with the principles advanced in his letter, eventually settling himself in Rosewater County, Indiana, his ancestral home. This return to his place of origin represents Eliot's personal pursuit of genesis, his desire to start over by subtly reshaping the way of life in this small town, which is presented as a microcosm of the larger fallen world. Vonnegut symbolically projects this sense of prelapsarian and postlapsarian Eden using two frames of reference often associated with Edenic and Golden Age myths—place and time.

Present-day Rosewater County is a sharply divided place composed essentially of the have's—the Rosewaters themselves—and the financial and emotional have-not's. The ancestors of many of the latter, we are told, were once utopian dreamers who lost everything they had in a canal scheme to link Chicago, Indianapolis, Rosewater County, and the Ohio River. The scheme, concocted by old Noah Rosewater, failed, and quite a few of the investors lost their farms, which Noah promptly bought up. Vonnegut provides a vivid and symbolically pregnant description of one of these bankrupted communities:

> A Utopian community in the southwest corner of the county, New Ambrosia, invested everything it had in the canal, and lost. They were Germans, communists and atheists who practiced group marriage, absolute truthfulness, absolute cleanliness, and absolute love. They were now scattered to the winds, like the worthless papers that represented their equity in the canal. . . . Their one contribution to the county that was still viable in Eliot's time was their brewery, which had become the home of Rosewater Golden Lager Ambrosia Beer. On the label of each can of beer was a picture of the heaven on earth the New Ambrosians had meant to build. The dream city had spires. The spires had lightning-rods. The sky was filled with cherubim.

The mythic overtones in this description are, of course, unmistakable, evoking variously Eden, the New Jerusalem, the realm of the Greek gods, and the American utopian ideal. By the time Eliot arrives here, though, nothing is left of these aspirations apart from a picture on a beer can made by a company that the Rosewaters now own. Indeed, the Rosewaters' monuments to wealth and position—a Parthenon, the Rosewater Saw Company, the county courthouse, the Samuel Rosewater Veterans' Memorial Park, the Rosewater Opera House, and the Rosewater mansion— represent the other segment of this fragmented microcosm, the utopian dreams of earlier inhabitants replaced with the capitalistic dreams of Noah Rosewater and his descendants. *Rosewater* is the name of one fragment of this ruined utopia; "all else was shithouses, shacks, alcoholism, ignorance, idiocy, and perversion."

Vonnegut employs the other mythic aspect—time—in an interesting way. In his description of the county seat, he chooses to dwell a bit on two buildings with clock towers, each tower bearing four clocks. The Rosewater Saw Company's four clocks, he says, are handless; and on the County courthouse, one clock is handless and the other three do not work. These details imply that time here in Rosewater has, in effect, been stalled, and that the quiet desperation of the inhabitants of this ruined utopian experiment goes on without change. Into this existential nightmare without end steps Eliot Rosewater, the worker of miracles, the bearer of the surname that has near divine status in terms of wealth and prestige and is anathema in terms of the greed and lack of compassion shown by his family. An artist whose tools are uncritical love and vast wealth, Eliot comes to effect change, to undo some of the damage done by his forebears' greed and pride, as well as to set time moving again and thus provide hope to the hopeless. As always in Vonnegut's novels, the alterations take a mythic backward turn away from self-centered "progress" and toward original purposes. In the eyes of the unloved, Eliot will come like a loving God, albeit a disturbed one, who comes to remake their world not so much physically as spiritually; and in this regard, we will see that he functions as both a Christ-like harbinger of better things to come and as a godlike maker of small universes.

Before we consider the mythic roles that Eliot comes to assume, however, it merits recalling that all of his activities are presented within a larger and more sinister context. The Rosewater Foundation's charter demands that any of its officers adjudged insane be removed and replaced with the next in line to the fortune. Though it is commonly supposed by the staff of the law firm representing the Rosewaters' interest that Eliot is a lunatic, no one there has actively tried to give legal credence to the playful rumor—no one, that is, until an avaricious newcomer, one Norman Mushari, joins the firm. Mushari is a diminutive man of Lebanese extraction, the son of a Brooklyn rug merchant, "the youngest, shortest, and by all odds the least Anglo-Saxon male employee in the firm"; a man with whom no one at work bothered much and whose chief purpose at the firm was to add "just a touch more viciousness." Mushari's crusade to have Eliot declared insane and to profit by representing the beneficiaries of the Rosewater trust (Fred Rosewater, a poor cousin to the heirless Eliot, living in Pisquontuit, Rhode Island) accords with the advice he once had from his favorite law professor that a lawyer should always be looking for situations where large amounts of money are about to change hands. Taking the advice one step further, Mushari is not only looking for such a situation but trying to create one; and in this regard, this new-generation American of immigrant stock recalls Eliot's own ancestor, Noah Rosewater, who also profited from the misfortunes of others. Moreover, just as Noah's name itself is ironically suggestive of the Old Testament dynastic figure through whom the Earth was repopulated, so Mushari equates his own activities to those of an admired biblical figure, another unlikely hero chosen by God to do wondrous things. The diminutive lawyer sees himself as something akin to the "brave little David about to slay Goliath."

Of course, no one else regards the gentle Eliot as being anything like Goliath. In fact, the playful nicknames the members of the firm give him— "The Nut," "The Saint," "The Holy Roller," and "John the Baptist" —would imply quite the contrary. Indeed, one of the principal tensions of the novel is between the destructive materialistic "wisdom" of people like Mushari and the gentle, lifesaving "folly" that Eliot displays. Unlike Noah and Samuel Rosewater and Norman Mushari, Eliot is equated for the most part with New Testament personages, all of whom work in the service of the new law of mercy, compassion, self-denial, and so on—"fools" by the world's standards. St. Paul's words about such folly are quite applicable to Eliot Rosewater:

> Divine folly is wiser than the wisdom of man, and divine weakness stronger than man's strength. My brothers, think what sort of people you are, whom God has called. Few of you are men of wisdom, by any human standard; few are powerful or highly born. Yet to shame the wise, God has chosen what the world counts folly, and to shame what is strong, God has chosen what the world counts weakness. He has chosen things low and contemptible, mere nothings to overthrow the existing order. And so there is no place for human pride in the presence of God. (1 Corinthians 1:25–29).

Although highly born and strong by the world's standards, Eliot nevertheless exemplifies the suppression of pride that Paul advocates here, thus qualifying for the title "divine fool." In keeping with this self-imposed folly, Eliot's personality and activity are equated with those of several New Testament figures, notably, the Good Samaritan, Christ, and John the Baptist.

The first of these associations is defined not only directly through his actions on behalf of the poor but also indirectly. Eliot's socialite wife, Sylvia, is at one point confined to a mental institution, suffering from what one psychiatrist calls *samaritrophia* or "hysterical indifference to the troubles of those less fortunate than oneself," "the suppression of an overactive conscience by the rest of the mind." Sylvia's bizarre condition is aggravated whenever she has contact with Eliot for his actions cause her to feel guilt, and she eventually concedes to Mushari and Eliot's father that, though Eliot is right to do the beautiful things he does, she herself is "simply not strong enough or good enough to be by his side anymore." When asked by Senator Rosewater the "secret thing" that these poor and unattractive people represent to Eliot, she reluctantly reveals it: "The secret is that they're human." Hence, like the Good Samaritan of the parable, Eliot acts to relieve human suffering for no better reason than simple compassion.

Likewise, Eliot's association with Christ derives from both his compassionate attitude and the "miracles" he works. One of Eliot's frequent callers on the telephone help line he has established in Rosewater County is Diana Moon Glampers, "a sixty-eight-year old virgin who, by almost anybody's standards, was too dumb to live." Diana is clearly unbalanced mentally, as evidenced by her belief that Eliot can cure chronic diseases and even control the lightning and thunder that she fears so much. In fact, her praise of Eliot echoes descriptions of Christ wherein he is said to have put off his divine glory for awhile and taken on the flesh:

> "You could have been so high and mighty in this world, that when you looked down on the plain, dumb, ordinary people of poor old Rosewater County, we would look like bugs. . . . You gave up everything a man is supposed to want, just to help the little people, and the little people know it. God bless you, Mr. Rosewater."

Despite her illogic and her hyperbole, Diana's praise of this extraordinary man rings quite true for what he has done is nothing short of mad and miraculous.

Finally, Eliot is ironically associated with John the Baptist both in name (that is, the playful nickname given to him by the staff at McAllister's law firm) and in deed. In a telephone conversation with his wife, Eliot says that he has been asked to baptize a pair of twins born in Rosewater County. Asked how he will do it, he responds:

> "Oh—I don't know. . . . Go over to her shack, I guess. Sprinkle some water on the babies, say, 'Hello, babies. Welcome to Earth. It's hot in the summer and cold in the winter. It's round and wet and crowded. At the outside, babies, you've got about a hundred years here. There's only one rule that I know of, babies—:

> "'God damn it, you've got to be kind.'"

Prior to saying this, Eliot expresses uncertainty as to why the twins' mother chose him to perform the religious rite since, he asserts, nothing he did could count in Heaven. The reader, however, might well disagree with his claim. Like John the Baptist, the saint who dwells in the wilderness, dressed in a rough coat of camel's hair, subsisting on locusts and wild honey—indeed, like all the holy "nuts" with whom he is figuratively equated—Eliot is a man crying in the wilderness, crying against the tide of greed and hypocrisy that has swept over America, crying the only message he finds worth hearing: "God damn it, you've got to be kind." If that message does not count heavily in Heaven, then none does.

Again, this injunction to kindness is delivered within a sinister context, since Mushari is eavesdropping on this conversation between Eliot and his wife. The lawyer's intent is to gather evidence that "Eliot's lunacy was not stabilized, but was about to make the great leap forward into religion." As such, this context proves to be troubling, for Mushari's search after evidence of Eliot's madness has its effect on the reader as well, prompting us to seek after signs of that madness. And, though we know that Eliot does not have any obsessions with religion, there are signs of mental disturbance presented throughout the novel. We know, for instance, that he is depressed most of the time, and even guilt-ridden over two incidents from his past. The first is the death of his mother in a boating accident for which he blames himself. The other is a wartime accident. Thinking he was killing German soldiers, he later discovered that the three men he killed—two old men and an adolescent—were actually volunteer firemen. This unfortunate error initially caused him to attempt suicide and later haunts him throughout his life. Thus, when we learn that Eliot has special affection for volunteer fire departments, we must place that affection within this unhappy context. Finally, there is Eliot's love of science fiction, particularly the works of one Kilgore Trout, the relatively obscure author of eighty-seven sci-fi novels, whom Eliot eventually meets and who aids immeasurably in Eliot's quest after meaning in life. This admiration for science fiction, which Eliot claims is due to the bold originality and caring attitude of its writers, might also be regarded as evidence, albeit circumstantial, of Eliot's desire for escape from the horrifying guilt he feels. In sum, it might well be argued, as some commentators have, that the eventual failure of Eliot's social activism, owing to his mental breakdown, was inevitable given the various obsessions, guilts, and other psychiatric disturbances that Eliot manifests.

I think, however, that such is not the case; and Vonnegut goes well out of his way to show the validity of Eliot's viewpoint, making him perhaps one of the most endearing of his protagonists. For one thing, there is the matter of overall context. The fact is that we do not judge fictional characters merely by bringing to the fiction our own moral standards. Rather, to a large extent, we judge them in relation to the circumstances in which they are placed. For instance, Fitzgerald's Gatsby would not be a very admirable character by conventional moral standards. Yet, by comparison to the hypocrisy of those with whom he interacts, matched with the narrator's sympathetic assessment of him, Fitzgerald manages to turn him into a protagonist for whom we can feel pity and admiration. So it is with Eliot Rosewater. In another context we might well judge Eliot to be, at best, a pathetic malcontent; at worst, a deluded and selfish opportunist. However, Vonnegut deliberately places his protagonist within a milieu where no one is morally superior to him, however troubled he might be. Indeed, his troubled mind may even be regarded as evidence that, unlike his distinguished forebears, Eliot has a well-developed conscience. Indeed, we would not have Eliot emulate his pietistic father or his socialite wife; we would not have Mushari succeed in his attempt at "the violent overthrow of the Rosewater Foundation"; we would not have Eliot "cured" of his obsessions and retreat to his safe and secure existence.

Even more explicitly, Vonnegut eventually brings Kilgore Trout himself onto the scene—the scene in this case being the mental hospital where Eliot is finally taken. Sent for by Senator Rosewater to help Eliot prepare for the sanity hearing that Mushari has arranged, Trout assesses the situation in ways that please both Eliot's father and the reader. Trout boldly defends virtually everything that Eliot has done. He argues that Eliot's social work in Rosewater County was nothing less than "possibly the most important social experiment of all time"—loving those who have no use. He also defends Eliot's love of volunteer fire departments on the grounds that they are "almost the only examples of enthusiastic unselfishness to be seen in the land [because] they rush to the rescue of any human being, and count not the cost." Eliot's father is delighted with these interpretations, which he regards as little more than public relations ploys, though he does acknowledge that Trout is, for his own part, telling the truth. And it is that truth, which we have suspected all along, Eliot's mental troubles notwithstanding, that vindicates Eliot, not in legalistic terms but in moral ones, the only ones that count ultimately. For all his righteous posturing, Senator Rosewater cannot comprehend his son's genuine righteousness; and when he tries to explain what Eliot might have learned form his social experiment, the senator can speak only in inane platitudes, saying that Eliot learned not to drink too much and to play god to the slobbering poor. Trout, on the other hand, sees the profound meanings implied in Eliot's altruism. "Thanks to the example of Eliot Rosewater," he asserts, "millions upon millions of people may learn to love and help whomever they see." As John May suggests, Trout has thus served his function as "Eliot's prophet, not to mention Vonnegut's mouthpiece," and as such, he has prepared the way for our recognition of Eliot's God-like status in the novel. Quite appropriately, Trout's last word summarizes all that Eliot has made possible: "Joy."

Quite significantly, Vonnegut chooses to end *Rosewater* with an ambiguous but nevertheless telling touch. Acknowledging all of the children said to be his in Rosewater County, Eliot orders his attorney to make them his legal heirs, an order that is couched in familiar terms indeed:

> "Let their names be Rosewater from this moment on. And tell them that their father loves them, no matter what they may turn out to be. And tell them—" Eliot fell silent, raised his tennis racket as though it were a magic wand.
>
> "And tell them," he began again, "to be fruitful and multiply."

As he delivers these words, Eliot is standing within the walled garden of a mental hospital, a place Vonnegut subtly and figuratively likens to the Garden of Eden amid the chaos that surrounds it and out of which it was made. Eliot awakens in this place after a black out "as black as what lay beyond the ultimate rim of the universe," seeing, as if for the first time, dappled sunshine and hearing a bird singing from up in a sycamore tree. Now, dressed in tennis whites that ironically recall the whiteness associated with God, Eliot confidently delivers words that faithfully echo the divine injunction to procreate. In effect, Eliot has at last found the Genesis that he has been pursuing for so long. Flying in the face of his father's vacuous platitude about not playing God, he does, in fact, take on something like the divine role, using his own considerable powers and resources to recreate the world in his own image, an image that places generosity of spirit over pride, altruism over self-interest, love over indifference.

By and large, critics have not been favorably disposed toward this concluding scene. Robert Uphaus argues that "in the face of American history, his gestures amount to nothing more than noble posturing." The raised tennis racket serves both as a symbol of Eliot's upper-class position and as a sign that magic wands do not exist. Likewise, Joyce Nelson maintains that money alone will not improve the lives of the beneficiaries and that "Eliot Rosewater's final gesture seems one of empty heroics." Richard Giannone observes that Eliot's defeat proves that Americans are too weak to be loved and that "one is left with the impression that Vonnegut's fatalism outweighs his sense of moral altruism." Stanley Schatt writes that "the very fact that he echoes Genesis in this final proclamation may well indicate that Eliot is taking the first step toward creating a new and hopefully better world." And yet, Schatt, too, is uncomfortable with that gesture. "It is very difficult, if not impossible," he concludes, "to determine whether he is sane or not at this point."

In the end, I think, the question of Eliot's sanity is no longer relevant, nor is the question of what money by itself can do for the poor, nor, for that matter, are the facts of American history and sociology. The gesture is all. Eliot Rosewater has found a means to do what each of Vonnegut's protagonists, sane or otherwise, are engage in doing. In his small way, he is remaking the world, reestablishing an Edenic existence of sorts—not with himself as Adam in this case, but as a benevolent and self-effacing god. In Milton's *Paradise Lost*, one of the most disturbing sights that Satan beholds is the love that Adam and Eve share. "Sight hateful, sight tormenting!" he cries inwardly, "thus these two / Imparadis't in one another's arms / the happier *Eden*." In his own way, Eliot makes such a paradise in Rosewater County, where the example of uncritical love becomes the foundation for a new world, a new Eden.

CHARLES BERRYMAN

Vonnegut's Comic Persona in Breakfast of Champions

When an author becomes a character in his own fiction, the traditional result is some form of autobiography. In post-modern fiction the author is more apt to pass through the looking glass into his own creation in order to question the very nature of his art. If the author becomes a naive character, bewildered and lost in his own novel, the result is comedy and satire. No one has presented this aspect of postmodern fiction with more comic delight than Kurt Vonnegut in *Breakfast of Champions.*

Vonnegut was unhappy with his brief venture into drama and television in the early 1970s because in a film "the author always vanishes." Vonnegut's desire to be a character in all his works prompted his return to a narrative form with more scope for self-revelation and parody. *Breakfast of Champions,* largely written by 1971 but not published until 1973, is a novel in which the comic persona of the author holds conversations with himself: "'This is a very bad book you're writing,' I said to myself . . . 'I know,' I said." No longer content with the limited autobiographical preface common in his earlier books, Vonnegut now introduces himself as a character to observe and participate in the climax of the story. Suddenly the author appears wearing dark glasses in the cocktail lounge of the Holiday Inn where he has assembled the chief characters for their violent interaction.

From *Critical Essays on Kurt Vonnegut,* edited by Robert Merrill. © 1990 by Robert Merrill.

Vonnegut's appearance in his seventh novel is a natural step in the evolution of his remarkable career. A few years earlier the dark glasses would have been unnecessary—who would have recognized him? In the middle of the 1960s Vonnegut's first four novels and his first collection of stories were all out of print. Despite fifteen years of work as a writer, Vonnegut found himself faced with oblivion. His situation was reminiscent of the career of Herman Melville a century before. If a writer achieves early success with a popular form—Melville with his romances of the South Pacific or Vonnegut with his science fiction—how can he attract a new audience when his craft matures and his metaphysical vision deepens? The skeptical themes and experimental forms of Melville's best novels only found a receptive public decades after his death. Vonnegut was very apprehensive about suffering the same eclipse. The specter of a prolific and misunderstood novelist haunted his imagination in the 1960s. It appeared in his novels as the forlorn and embittered science-fiction writer, Kilgore Trout.

At the nadir of his expectations in 1965 Vonnegut decided upon two strategies that might rescue his career from the fate of his fictional novelist. He decided to separate himself from the label of science fiction and to promote his own image in the public media as often as possible. Consequently he announced in the *New York Times Book Review*: "I have been a sore-head occupant of a file drawer labeled 'science fiction' . . . and I would like out!" He also devoted a considerable time to first-person journalism. Readers of magazines like *Esquire*, *Life*, *Playboy*, and *Mademoiselle* were offered Vonnegut's latest opinions on everything from astronauts to mass murderers. Many of his journalistic ventures were designed to impress the public with his image as a social critic and satirist, but the saving grace of this journalism is its mocking tone and occasional self-parody. His piece on the Maharishi Mahesh Yogi, for example, is entitled "Yes, We Have No Nirvanas."

In 1965 Vonnegut also began two years of residence at the University of Iowa Writers Workshop. For the first time he was in daily contact with students and critics who pressed him for explanations about his craft. While such academic debate often paralyzes less experienced writers, it proved to be a significant catalyst for Vonnegut's mature fiction. When his third novel *Mother Night*, was reissued in 1966, Vonnegut decided to add an autobiographical preface describing his experience during the bombing of Dresden. Two years later he wrote a personal introduction to his collection of stories, *Welcome to the Monkey House*, in which he explored the relationship of life and art. His next novel was *Slaughterhouse-Five* with its opening chapter in the form of an author's confession. Step by step Vonnegut was moving himself onto the stage of his fiction.

Vonnegut seldom explores a possibility for his art without soon beginning to parody its form. The next step for his progressive revelation of self was therefore the self-mocking portrait of the author as character in *Breakfast of Champions*. By the time this novel appeared in 1973 the author was experiencing all the pressures of literary success. His brief residence among the academics, not to mention his advertisements of himself in popular journals, were beginning to pay remarkable dividends. His long-anticipated war novel, *Slaughterhouse-Five*, was welcomed in 1969 by scores of favorable reviews. Vonnegut thus began to enjoy the second audience that Melville never lived to see. The full emergence of Vonnegut as a literary celebrity in the early 1970s provided him with a new public image just ripe for satire in *Breakfast of Champions*. While he was receiving maximum exposure in the various public media, Vonnegut was also devising new ways of representing himself in fiction.

Vonnegut knew that his first novel of the 1970s would attract considerable publicity. Indeed, three book clubs were waiting to offer it as the featured selection. He also assumed that his new novel would be judged against the achievement of *Slaughterhouse-Five*. So much of Vonnegut's over-experience had gone into the writing of *Slaughterhouse-Five* that its audience and author alike must have been wondering what he could do next. The novel that comes after a major achievement has always been a special problem for American writers. After the publication of *Moby-Dick* in 1851, Melville's next and seventh novel was the ill-fated *Pierre*. After the success of *Slaughterhouse-Five* in 1969, Vonnegut was afraid that his next book, also a seventh novel, would disappoint his new audience. For a while he delayed publication of *Breakfast of Champions*. Moreover, he built a negative critical response into the book itself. Anticipating an audience now ready to chip away at his new fame and fortune, Vonnegut presents a comic image of the author dissatisfied with his own work and then attacked by a ravenous dog at the end of the book. The writer appears as a character in his own novel, not merely to conduct a dialogue with himself about the relationship of art and life, but also to deflect the charges of his audience. When the dog at the end of the book springs for the jugular vein of the author, our storyteller makes a comic leap over his rented automobile to safety. Vonnegut's personal thus escapes with his life, but at the same time a local tourist attraction known as *Moby-Dick* is being destroyed by industrial waste.

Vonnegut's appearance in his own novel also allows him to parody his reputation as a hip philosopher. Even his early books attracted a cult following eager to find metaphysical speculation. Vonnegut appealed to this audience by including various fantastic religions such as the Church of God the Utterly Indifferent in *The Sirens of Titan* or Bokononism in *Cat's Cradle*. Despite the comic thrust of his early metaphysical capers, Vonnegut was aware that some readers and critics were solemnly discussing his philosophy. No doubt he found the spectacle amusing. When academic critics began to claim with awe that "Vonnegut is wrestling with nothing less than the cosmological question," who could blame the novelist for laughing to himself? And he encouraged such discussion by scattering his views on almost every subject throughout the popular journals. During the late 1960s Vonnegut was almost always available for instant wisdom in press interviews, talk shows, commencement addresses, etc. What his audience didn't always perceive, however, was the amount of self-parody inherent in his public image. Vonnegut was performing in the spirit of Mark Twain, pretending to be profound, when all along the joke was on his audience. His metaphysical comedy bred a solemn debate among critics and disciples about his view of a "meaningful existence," and the debate was often held in a nonsense language. "In the post-apocalyptic void," wrote one critic, "all identity is adventitious." The language of critical discussion thus entered the world of chrono-synclastic infundibula without noticing its own comic echo.

Although he may have enjoyed hearing himself praised as "the foremost serious writer in America today," Vonnegut was experiencing the bitter-sweet frustration of being praised for the wrong reasons. When would he be recognized as the foremost comic writer? Vonnegut also began to worry about the critics who were seeing through his metaphysical charade without recognizing its comic potential. Leslie Fiedler, for example, was remarking in 1970 that Vonnegut's own spiritual age is late adolescence. The title of Fiedler's article, "The Divine Stupidity of Kurt Vonnegut," and the fact that it appeared in *Esquire*, the home of some of Vonnegut's own writing, were both disconcerting. But a far worse attack was published the next year by Charles Samuels in the *New Republic*. Samuels declared that Vonnegut "can tell us nothing worth knowing except what his rise itself indicates: ours is an age in which adolescent ridicule can become a mode of upward mobility." Samuels at least did not take Vonnegut's metaphysical performance with great solemnity—"a sententious old salt in ontological drag"—but he still implied that Vonnegut would like his philosophy to be accepted without irony. Nothing could be further from the truth. Vonnegut decided to counter such false impressions by increasing the self-parody in his next novel, *Breakfast of Champions*, and by placing such misunderstandings at the very center of his narrative.

Breakfast of Champions is about a novelist named Kilgore Trout who is invited to attend an art conference in Midland City. There he meets his potential audience, Dwayne Hoover, who rapidly becomes insane after one reading of a Trout novel. The mad rampage of Hoover, who injures eleven people and bites off the end of Trout's finger, is a mock description of the conduct of Vonnegut's own audience and its penchant for biting the hand that feeds it.

Kilgore Trout, familiar to readers of earlier Vonnegut novels, achieves a new significance in *Breakfast of Champions*. Although he travels to the art conference in order to reveal the face of failure to a naive and uncomprehending audience, he unexpectedly meets his creator and is granted ironic freedom. It is even reported that Trout will soon receive a Nobel Prize. The public will read his science fiction as if it were true, and he will be awarded the Nobel Prize for Medicine. With such bravado, Vonnegut is simultaneously mocking the solemn incomprehension of his own audience and exorcising the specter of a failed career. Better the wrong Nobel Prize than none at all!

Trout's fiction is described as "solipsistic whimsy," and the same label has been applied by more than one critic to Vonnegut's novel. The criticism is encouraged by the tone and style of the book, which readers often find exasperating and silly. The tone is deliberately simpleminded. The persona of the author is pretending to tell the story as if he were reporting events on a distant and dying planet. The style includes drawings by the author of such obvious things as a light switch, a cow, and a hamburger. "I've often thought," Vonnegut once declared, "there ought to be a manual to hand to little kids, telling them what kind of planet they're on, why they don't fall off it, how much time they've probably got here . . . I tried to write one once. It was called *Welcome to Earth*. But I got stuck on explaining why we don't fall off the planet." Unfortunately, *Breakfast of Champions* often sounds like such a manual, and it is not surprising that so many readers have resented being addressed in such a manner.

The strategy of the novel, however, is less sentimental and patronizing than at first it seems. Vonnegut's satire depends on a perception of the difference between the author and his naive persona. Although the persona does conform with some of the known facts of Vonnegut's life—date of birth, details about parents, and concerns about mental health—the persona is an obtuse, comic self-parody of the novelist.

Vonnegut reveals the identity of the persona very clearly in the novel: "What do I myself think of this particular book? I feel lousy about it, but I always feel lousy about my books. My friend Knox Burger said one time that a certain cumbersome novel 'read as though it had been written by Philboyd Studge.' That's who I think I am when I write what I am seemingly programmed to write." The same voice says a paragraph later, "I am programmed at fifty to perform childishly." The first-person pronoun is prominent, but who is the "I" speaking to us? Vonnegut happens to be fifty at the time, but this preface to the novel is signed by "Philboyd Studge." The comic name belongs to the narrator who serves as a self-parody of Vonnegut, but the name comes from a short story by Saki (Hector Hugh Munro) about the perversity of public taste and the ingratitude suffered by a poor artist.

Saki's brief tale, "Filboid Studge, The Story of a Mouse That Helped," tells about an artist who encourages a huge demand for an awful breakfast cereal merely by calling it "Filboid Studge." Vonnegut's *Breakfast of Champions* is not only named after a famous advertising slogan for a breakfast cereal, a registered trademark for Wheaties, it is also narrated by Philboyd Studge, the name created in Saki's story to sell the most unpalatable breakfast cereal of all time. The poor artist in the story advertises the cereal by drawing a picture of hell where a fashionable public is tempted by the cereal just beyond their reach. Filboid Studge is thus the image of what the damned public wants but cannot enjoy, and the artist who gives them the image remains at the end of the story unrewarded. The perversity of public taste and the ingratitude faced by an artist are among the themes presented and mocked in *Breakfast of Champions*.

The style and tone of Vonnegut's novel are consistent with the comic persona called "Philboyd Studge." His are the childish observations about common things. His are the drawings scrawled with a felt-tipped pen. But who wants to read a novel told and illustrated by the namesake of a breakfast cereal? Even if Vonnegut can be successfully separated from Philboyd Studge, the responsibility for creating the self-parody still belongs with the novelist. What advantages, if any, come from having Philboyd Studge serve as the narrator of *Breakfast of Champions*?

If satire depends upon irony, perhaps it is helpful to have a naive storyteller who seems to know less about things than either the author or the audience. This is the familiar strategy of *Gulliver's Travels*, and the adventures of Gulliver are not far removed from the comic accidents of Philboyd Studge. Both serve as first-person narrators telling us about their experiences that neither can fully understand or control. Gulliver's assumed superiority to the King of the Brobdingnagians is just as ironic as the conceit of Philboyd Studge. Gulliver's admiration for the Houyhnhnms is just as ridiculous as the naiveté of Vonnegut's narrator. The misadventures of both storytellers—captured by the Lilliputians or injured at the Holiday Inn—are comic and absurd. The humor comes from our recognition that Lemuel Gulliver and Philboyd Studge, despite their pretensions of superiority, are still quintessential Yahoos. The reputation of Jonathan Swift as the greatest satirist in the English language is commonly accepted even though critics still disagree about how to distinguish Swift and Gulliver and how to interpret Gulliver's final response to the Houyhnhnms. Such critical problems are inherent in satire. Thus it is hardly surprising that contemporary readers have difficulty when it comes to separating Vonnegut from his persona and interpreting the narrator's response. Gulliver's final resentment over the pride of the Yahoos is just as ironic as the last tear shed by Vonnegut's narrator over a fate he cannot understand.

Once the narrator of *Breakfast of Champions* is viewed as a naive story-teller, the many conversations in the novel about the very process of writing are understandable in a new context. When the narrator says to himself, "this is a very bad book you're writing," we should hear the comic despair of Philboyd Studge unable to live up to the standards of the Houyhnhnms. If the dissatisfaction were Vonnegut's, there would be no excuse for publishing the book. But if the feeling belongs to the comic persona, than Vonnegut succeeds in mocking the fears and pretensions of his fictional author.

Vonnegut's narrator assumes a self-indulgent tone at the beginning when he announces: "This book is my fiftieth birthday present to myself." The birthday celebration is viewed as a time to take stock of the many characters in the author's head: "I think I am trying to clear my head of all the junk in there . . . I'm throwing out characters from my other books, too. I'm not going to put on any more puppet shows." Vonnegut is mocking that decisive moment in an author's career when he feels ready to abandon his cast of characters. The best examples in English literature are Shakespeare allowing Prospero to dismiss the "elves of hills, brooks, standing lakes and groves" and W. B. Yeats concluding that his circus animals will no longer be on show.

Prospero's words, which echo Medea in Ovid, are both proud and apologetic. Despite his references to "weak masters" and "rough magic," the poetry reverberates with the proud knowledge of his accomplishments. Prospero has imitated the power of the gods— "to the dread rattling thunder / Have I given fire and rifted Jove's stout oak / With his own bolt." Shakespeare is about to retire from the London stage, and it is hardly a time for modesty about his "potent art." Vonnegut, however, has no intentions of ending his career, and the farewell gestures of his comic persona are both vain and disingenuous. Vonnegut's narrator has very limited power to create or destroy. He is trapped and victimized in the world of his own characters. Any attempt to assume godlike power leads quickly to a pratfall. The more he tries to clear his head, the faster the junk inside appears to multiply.

His gesture of dismissal—"I'm not going to put on any more puppet shows"—sounds closer to the disappearing circus animals of Yeats, but Vonnegut's narrator is merely exhibiting a false bravado at age fifty, and not the final realization that old themes and characters can no longer be summoned when it is time to "lie down where all the ladders start, / In the foul rag-and-bone shop of the heart." Vonnegut's naive persona hides behind his dark glasses at the Holiday Inn and hardly begins to approach his own heart. The comic irony of the narrator is multiplied by the self-indulgent tone of his decision to celebrate his own birthday and the self-deluded gesture of dismissing his own characters.

The full comedy of the author attempting to dismiss his characters occurs near the end of *Breakfast of Champions*. The author in a rented Plymouth Duster is chasing after his most famous creation: "'Whoa! I'm a friend!' I said . . . 'Mr. Trout,' I said from the unlighted interior of the car, 'you have nothing to fear. I bring you tidings of great joy.'" The divine pretensions of the author are immediately mocked when he attempts to turn on the light and merely succeeds in activating the windshield wipers. When it comes to the climactic moment of freeing his character, he invokes the memory of Count Tolstoi freeing his serfs and Thomas Jefferson freeing his slaves, but the great emancipation ironically backfires. When the author says, "Arise, Mr. Trout, you are free, you are *free*," the character suddenly appears to have the face of the author's father, and his last words are: "*Make me young, make me young, make me young!*" The result of bringing the comic author face to face with the image of his own father is to undercut his pride as a creator. He has no more power to set his creation free than he does to make his father young. Indeed, if the character is the father of the author, then the very tables of creation have been turned. Vonnegut, of course, is the father of both the character and the comic author, and the disillusionment of both in the novel completes Vonnegut's self-parody and his satire of the vain delusions of narcissistic authors.

If the chief delusion of an author is the attempt to assume divine creative power, Vonnegut deliberately mocks his comic persona for indulging such pretensions. We should laugh at the vanity of the narrator when he modestly announces: "I was on a par with the Creator of the Universe there in the dark in the cocktail lounge." We might also recall that the same narrator has been complaining about the incompetence, the cruelty, and the indifference of the Creator at frequent intervals throughout the novel. He has often referred to a God who moves in disastrous ways creating tornadoes and tidal waves or destroying a whole galaxy for the mere pleasure of the fireworks. Thus when the narrator introduces himself as being "on a par with the Creator," he is vainly assuming some rather dubious credentials.

The dialogue between the comic author and the bewildered Kilgore Trout is a wonderful example of baffled condescension and suspicious distrust. The author playing God in his rented car has promised "tidings of great joy," but Trout's response to the good news is a noncommital "Um." Frustrated by the ungrateful response, the author says, "If I were in your spot, I would certainly have lots of questions." Trout's wary reply is "Do you have a gun?" Trout has good reason to be suspicious of anyone approaching him in a car. Earlier in the novel he was "kidnapped by pure evil in a white

Oldsmobile" and left unconscious after losing his money. How can Kilgore Trout be certain that the author in the rented Plymouth is not a member of the Pluto gang ready to strike again?

The narrator says that he wants to bless his creation with the gift of harmony: " 'Mr. Trout, I love you,' I said gently. 'I have broken your mind to pieces. I want to make it whole. I want you to feel wholeness and inner harmony such as I have never allowed you to feel before'." And what does Trout see in the hand of his benevolent creator? An apple! There is no sign that Vonnegut's comic author in the role of God recognizes what will come from the fruit he so kindly offers. Unknowingly, he is placing his favorite character in the same position that is described in Trout's novel *Now It Can Be Told.* This science-fiction novel is written in the form of a letter from the Creator of the Universe to "the only creature in the entire Universe who has free will." When this message from the Creator was read by Dwayne Hoover, who was just insane enough to believe it, the result was his mad rampage through the Holiday Inn. When the apple of freedom is offered to Kilgore Trout by his naive creator, who believes the apple is "a symbol of wholeness and harmony and nourishment," the poor science fiction writer thinks his creator is merely playing one final joke upon him. The offer of freedom is therefore met with the desperate wish that all the knowledge and experience of the tempting fruit could be withdrawn— *"Make me young, make me young, make me young!"*

Vonnegut, of course, is the creator of the comic author, who in turn plays God and pretends to be the creator of Kilgore Trout, who in turn is the author of *Now It Can Be Told*, which describes the Creator of the Universe making the promise of free will. "My books," Vonnegut has said, "are essentially mosaics made up of whole bunch of little chips; and each chip is a joke." The humor reflects on all the authors in and out of Vonnegut's book who assume the guise of divine power only to discover the knowledge of evil that comes from their best intentions. The last joke is on author and characters alike—the tidings of great joy become paradise lost.

PETER FREESE

Kurt Vonnegut's Slaughterhouse-Five; or, How to Storify an Atrocity

During the night of February 13, 1945, three waves of British and American bombers dropped about 3,000 tons of bombs, mostly incendiaries, upon the residential center of Dresden, a virtually undefended city with at best a marginal strategic significance. In this night, the ancient capital of Saxony was filled to overflowing, since to its 630,000 permanent residents were added about 30,000 prisoners of war of diverse nationalities and at least 600,000 refugees fleeing from the advancing Red Army, who had neither a proper home nor a chance to seek the protection of an air-raid shelter. With their attack, the Allied Forces staged an unprecedented spectacle of annihilation, which turned an overcrowded city into "one big flame [that] ate everything organic, everything that would burn" and exterminated about 135,000 helpless civilians within the space of 14 hours and ten minutes.

A young man who survived this "greatest massacre in European history" and saw how a raging firestorm changed "the loveliest city" into a smouldering moonscape and killed almost twice as many victims as the atomic bomb dropped upon Hiroshima, was the American POW Kurt Vonnegut, Jr. It took him "twenty-three years" and several apocalyptic novels to exorcise this traumatic encounter with what Lifton aptly defined as "the increasing gap we face between our technological capacity for perpetrating atrocities and our imaginative ability to confront their full actuality." The

From *Historiographic Metafiction in Modern American and Canadian Literature*, edited by Bernd Engler and Kurt Müller. © 1994 by Ferdinand Schöningh, Paderborn.

eventual result of Vonnegut's attempt to come to terms with his Dresden experience was his "anti-war book" *Slaughterhouse-Five, or The Children's Crusade* (1969), of which he says it was "a therapeutic thing" and made him "a different person." The painful gestation of this unique novel can hardly surprise, since any writer who tries to reconstruct a historical atrocity of such unimaginable proportions by means of traditional fictional strategies, that is, by storifying the event through an individual narrative perspective, is bound to fail, for the sheer number of casualties transcends the limits of personal empathy. A historical novel about the destruction of Dresden, therefore, is not only beset by the genre-specific problems of recreating the past through the epistemological limitations of the present, but also defeated by the very limits of the human imagination. This is why Vonnegut has to resort to unheard-of narrative strategies and why *Slaughterhouse-Five* is a tale that defies all generic classifications and introduces strange new ways of dealing with the grievous lessons of history.

Vonnegut's "Dresden story" is a slim novel consisting of ten chapters that vary greatly in length and seem to be rather arbitrarily divided. The first and the last chapter function as a narrative frame and offer a built-in manual of instruction for the puzzled reader. In the opening chapter, Vonnegut concatenates seemingly irrelevant autobiographical fragments in what appears to be a wilfully random way and reports on the extreme difficulties he had in writing his book. Here, then, he follows a well-worn strategy of modernist fiction by making the difficult genesis of the text a part of it. In the concluding chapter he pursues a different strategy; he mixes episodes from his own life with passages about his protagonist's adventures, concluding the text with the latter's journey through the smoking remnants of Dresden. The narrative frame is not fully closed, for the inset narration juts out beyond it and the text that opens in the factual world ends on a fictional plane. Not only is the traditional technique of the frame tale irritatingly modified, but Vonnegut also intrudes quite unabashedly as an actor or witness into the inset story and thereby contributes once more to the bewildering blending of two narrative strands with different degrees of 'reality' and of two time levels which convention demands should be clearly distinguished, namely those of the narrated action and the narrative process. Twice a particular event is authenticated by a sudden "I was there"; when a prisoner exclaims "Oz" upon his first sight of beautiful Dresden, this is followed by an unexpected "that was I"; and when a sick POW wails that he has excreted everything but his brain, one reads "That was I. That was me. That was the author of this book."

These sudden illusion-breaking intrusions are not the only proof of the pervasive presence of a constantly manipulating narrator. The laconic refrain

"So it goes," that punctuates the text in more than a 100 instances, keeps the reader steadily aware that the text is the highly subjective product of a troubled mind at work behind it, and when new characters are introduced, the perspective leaves the protagonist's *persona* and switches to an Olympian point of view. Moreover, Vonnegut reveals his presence through sweeping value judgments such as "Like so many Americans, she was trying to construct a life that made sense from things she found in gift shops," and he betrays his ironic distance through irreverent comments, as when he observes that the diarrhea of the coughing prisoners is "in accordance with the Third Law of Motion according to Sir Isaac Newton." In statements like that about Billy finding himself once more engaged "in the argument with his daughter, with which this tale began," he explains his narrative procedures, and in observations like "there are almost no characters in this story, and almost no dramatic confrontations, because most of the people in it are so sick" he reflects upon the problems he faces in storifying his intractable *sujet*. Taken together, his bewildering blending of fact and fiction, his disturbing mixture of different time levels, his illusion-breaking intrusions, his deft manipulation of the point of view, his sweeping value judgments and biting comments, his careful explanations and bothered reflections make the narrator a mediating instance that is insistently present between the protagonist and the reader, prevents the latter's identification with the former, and makes the customary quasi-pragmatic reception of the novel impossible.

Vonnegut fictionalizes his Dresden experience by making a piteous optician from Ilium, New York, the protagonist of his novel, and when he christens this anti-hero Billy Pilgrim, he evokes Bunyan's *The Pilgrim's Progress* and insinuates that Billy is a contemporary Everyman on his burdensome journey through an earthly valley of tears. Like his creator, Billy was born in 1922, and he will be murdered in Chicago on February 13, 1976, seven years after the publication of the novel and on the anniversary of the Dresden firestorm. This preposterous and grotesquely passive man, who is otherwise a very ordinary being, is "unstuck in time" and thus possesses the extraordinary ability to travel into the past and the future and to spend time on the extragalactic planet Tralfamadore. Since Wells's *The Time Machine*, the motif of time-travel is a stock-in-trade element of science fiction, but to conservative readers its irreverent application to a historical subject as serious as the Dresden massacre must seem glaringly inappropriate. However, this violation of generic conventions in a self-reflexive tale that blends autobiography with realistic narration, satirical exaggeration, and "science fiction of an obviously kidding sort" is by no means the only problem, since it is impossible to decide whether Billy really travels in time or only hallucinates his extragalactic journeys, whether *Slaughterhouse-Five* is a science-fiction novel or a novel with a mentally disturbed protagonist who is haunted by science-fiction fantasies.

On the one hand, the narrator insists on the 'reality' of Billy's time-travels through such statements as "Billy Pilgrim was having a delightful hallucination. [. . .] This wasn't time-travel. It had never happened, never would happen." or "Billy [. . .] dreamed millions of things, some of them true. The true things were time-travel." On the other hand, Billy experiences war and captivity as an unbearable ordeal, suffers a first crack-up in the prison camp and another "nervous breakdown" as a student, is the only heavily injured survivor of an airplane crash, and loses his wife in a freakish incident. Released from hospital with "a terrible scar across the top of his skull," his is "quiet for a while" and then all of a sudden begins to spread his Tralfamadorian gospel. This sounds suspiciously like the biography of a man who develops schizophrenia as what Laing calls "a special strategy [invented] in order to live in an unlivable situation," and such a reading seems confirmed by the fact that after his return from Dresden Billy spends some time in a mental hospital, where a fellow patient, Eliot Rosewater, the mad protagonist of Vonnegut's previous novel *God Bless You, Mr. Rosewater*, introduces him to the work of the science-fiction writer Kilgore Trout and makes him read *The Big Board*, a novel that lays out the scenario of his later adventures on Tralfamadore. Thus, *Slaughterhouse-Five* leaves it vexingly open whether it is Vonnegut who uses science-fiction strategies to distance the terror of Dresden or Billy who employs them to flee into a more hospitable fantasy world. But by pointing out that Eliot Rosewater and Billy Pilgrim "were trying to re-invent themselves and their universe" and that in this attempt "science fiction was a big help," the text provides the crucial *raison d'être* for linking the Dresden firestorm with science-fiction motifs.

Vonnegut employs the science-fiction level of his tale as one of several generic conventions through which to search for the meaning of the Dresden massacre. The puzzling interplay of these conventions, which are both realistic and fantastic, mimetic and anti-mimetic, not only serves as the formal equivalent of the insight that an atrocity like the Dresden firestorm defies any traditional storification, but it also abolishes the customary distinction between fiction and historiography. *Slaughterhouse-Five* shows that the difference between the historian's discovery of pre-existing realities and the novelist's invention of homemade stories is not one of principle but one of accentuation only, since historiography, too, "pre-figures the historical field and constitutes it as a domain upon which to bring to bear the specific theories [it] will use to explain 'what was really happening in it.'" And Vonnegut is in a privileged position to drive home this decisive point, for he is a German-American who suffered from anti-German sentiments as a

Cornell student and then survived the destruction of Dresden by the Allies as an American soldier in German captivity and thus cannot but assume a mediating stance, which the text emplots by presenting Billy and his German guard, the *luck*less Werner *Gluck*, as "distant cousins." This is why Vonnegut, who approaches the destruction of Dresden from the points of view of both the victims and the victimizers, is immune against rashly taking sides and can unmask the official versions of the Dresden massacre as nothing but predictable and prejudiced fictions. In the introductory chapter, Vonnegut recalls with deceptive simplicity:

> I happened to tell a University of Chicago professor at a cocktail party about the raid as I had seen it, about the book I would write. He was a member of a thing called The Committee on Social Thought. And he told me about the concentration camps, and about how the Germans had made soap and candles out of the fat dead Jews and so on.
>
> All I could say was, "I know, I know, I know."

In the novel proper Billy Pilgrim experiences exactly the same situation, when after his airplane crash he shares a hospital room with Bertram Copeland Rumfoord. This prototypically 'successful' American is a famous "Harvard history professor" at work on "a one-volume history of the United States Army Air Corps in World War Two," and between him and Billy the following dialogue ensues:

> "It *had* to be done," Rumfoord told Billy, speaking of the destruction of Dresden.
> "I know," said Billy.
> "That's war."
> "I know. I'm not complaining."
> "It must have been hell on the ground."
> "It was," said Billy Pilgrim.
> "Pity the men who had to *do* it."
> "I do."
> "You must have had mixed feelings, there on the ground."
> "It was all right," said Billy.

These two scenes clearly show that every version of the past is conditioned by the needs and values of the person who holds it, but Vonnegut is not yet satisfied. He makes Rumfoord acquaint Billy with President Truman's announcement of the Hiroshima bomb and Irving's book about *The Destruction of Dresden*, and by lengthily quoting from these factual documents about massive air raids within his fictional recreation of the most murderous one, he further underscores his point. Truman's callous statement that "the force from which the sun draws its power has been loosed against those who brought war to the Far East" and that thus the victims of Pearl Harbor have rightfully retaliated by killing "71,379" Japanese civilians; Lieutenant General Eaker's incensed admonition that, in drawing the frightful picture of the civilians killed in Dresden, Irving should have remembered "that V-1's and V-2's were at the very time falling on England, killing civilian men, women, and children indiscriminately"; and Air Marshal Saundby's embarrassed admission that the "great tragedy" of Dresden was "one of those terrible things that sometimes happen in wartime, brought about by an unfortunate combination of circumstances" are all revealing rationalizations of mass murder. They range from the claim for moral superiority through the insistence on rightful revenge to the admission of logistic mistakes, and Eaker's version even insinuates that one can balance one atrocity against another and thus expiate guilt by mutual neutralization. This exercise in inhuman book-keeping is as ludicrous as the fact that "the twenty-seven-volume *Official History of the Army Air Force in World War Two*" contains "almost nothing [. . .] about the Dresden raid," because "the extent of the success had been kept a secret for many years after the war—a secret from the American people. It was no secret from the Germans, of course." The intra-textual confrontation of these official documents with Vonnegut's factual experience and Billy's fictional adventure convincingly demonstrates that 'fictions' are not at all limited to the realm of *belles lettres*, and it makes the puzzled reader muse with Richard Nixon in Robert Coover's *The Public Burning*: "Strange, the impact of History, the grip it had on us, yet it was nothing but words."

Billy Pilgrim has no mastery over his time-travels and thus "no control over where he is going next," and he experiences the 54 years of his life in a discontinuous and seemingly random sequence. Since the novel follows the erratic sequence of Billy's life as a "spastic in time," it liberates Vonnegut from the strictures of a linear plot and a logically unfolding chronology and allows him to unfold his tale in a "telegraphic-schizophrenic manner" (subtitle) by relating short experiential fragments like the pieces of a faultily assembled puzzle. On closer scrutiny, however, what seems like wilful disorder is revealed as a carefully designed texture, and readers who are conversant with the cinematographic techniques of hard cuts, associative fades, and artful montage, can impose order upon the narrative contingency through a process of sense-making co-authoring. In doing so, they not only detect an artfully executed deep structure, but also recognize that Vonnegut employs his unusual mode of presentation for the urgent purpose of escaping the yoke of narrative succession. But in contrast to his modernist predecessors, who experimented with similar means to manipulate the unfolding of psychological time only, Vonnegut maintains that chronological time, too, must not be treated as "the straight and uniform string of beads most people think it is," because "we do live our lives simultaneously." Consequently, he uses the science-fiction motif of time-travel to break up not only the subjective experience but also the objective measurement of time and thereby to spatialize his tale. This allows him to achieve three goals at once, namely, to relativize the official versions of a historical event by reconstructing it from an idiosyncratic point of view, to thematize contemporary problems through a subjective consciousness, and to extrapolate the possibilities of tomorrow from the potential of today. Consequently, his innovative tale is not only a self-reflexive inquiry into the impossibility of writing a historical novel, but it also demonstrates, through an artful interplay of its three levels, that both James Baldwin and E. L. Doctorow were right when they maintained that "the past is all that makes the present coherent" and that "there is no history except as it is composed."

As a tale that abolishes the customary distinction between fact and fiction and violates generic conventions as well as established rules of narration, *Slaughterhouse-Five* asks the reader to perform a rather demanding task. Since Vonnegut is well aware that literature "requires the audience to be a performer" and that therefore "the limiting factor is the reader," he provides detailed directions for use, and he does so in the introductory chapter, which is not the rambling melange of odd bits and pieces it seems to be, but an artful collage of literary quotations and autobiographical fragments that have subtle thematic relevance and serve as cryptic pointers at things to come. Among these elements are a postcard from the Dresden cab driver Gerhard Müller, a dirty limerick about "a young man from Stamboul," a circular song about Yon Yonson, an unidentified quotation from Horace, *Odes* II:14:1f., a passage from Charles Mackay's *Extraordinary Popular Delusions and the Madness of Crowds* of 1841, a paragraph from Mary Endell's *Dresden, History, Stage and Gallery* of 1908, a quotation within a quotation from Goethe's *Dichtung und Wahrheit*, three lines from Theodore Roethke's poem *Words for the Wind*, an observation from Ferdinand Céline's *Mort à Credit* as quoted from Erika Ostrovsky's *Céline and His Vision*, a passage from the Gideon Bible, namely Genesis 19:23-25, about the destruction of Sodom and Gomorrha, and the first and last sentences of *Slaughterhouse-Five* as a self-reflexive quotation from the novel within the novel. This odd string of references violates another generic distinction by closing the customary gap between 'high' and 'low,' since 'serious' authors from Horace to Roethke are invoked side by side with a popular doggerel and a dirty limerick. And the sheer number of these references attests to the importance of a narrative strategy that thrives on the blending of different discourses and that creates a multiply refracted intertextuality, which is further thickened by the fact that with Kilgore Trout, Eliot Rosewater, and Howard Campbell major characters from Vonnegut's earlier novels reappear and enlarge the referential horizon.

One would have to engage in a page-by-page reconstruction of Vonnegut's associative technique to reveal the cryptic functionality of these oddly self-reflexive references, but a single example must suffice to reveal the method behind the narrative madness and to illustrate the degree to which *Slaughterhouse-Five* is an imaginative re-processing of earlier discourses. When Roland Weary, who is certainly very weary but by no means a Roland, escapes from the unbearable reality of war into his private fantasy world of the Three Musketeers, he tells himself about the heroic deeds of these legendary heroes, and the whole passage turns out to be a word-by-word repetition of the earlier quotation from Mackay's book, in which he dilates upon the irrationality of the romantic literature about the Crusades. This subversive repetition plus variation exposes Weary's fantasies as a timeless human aberration, but Vonnegut is not content with this telling refraction. Therefore, he once more undercuts the patriotic heroism of the Three Musketeers by making a sensation-seeking secretary inquire about the gruesome death of a man while "eating a Three Musketeers Candy Bar" and by having Billy's obese fiancée sit at the bedside of her broken-down lover and munch "a Three Musketeers Candy Bar."

In more general terms, the metafictional strategies which the introductory chapter offers for a successful co-authoring of the inset story and an imaginative reconstruction of the meaning of history are the *regressus ad infinitum* as a narrative equivalent of epistemological doubt, the blurring between fact and fiction as an expression of ontological insecurity, and the cumulation of multiply cross-referenced repetitions as an indication of man's imprisonment in the ruling linguistic discourses. It is a 'postmodern' truism that serious storytellers can no longer depict a shared reality and thus are incapable of recreating a historic event 'as it really was.' Confronted with competing realities that depend upon the perceptions and value systems of their individual projectors, Vonnegut takes recourse to the science-fiction strategy of the Martian perspective and makes use of the opposition between Earthlings and Tralfamadorians to demonstrate the dubiousness of the ontological distinction between fact and fiction. Another consequence of such radical idealism, convincingly thematized in Borges' *ficciones*, is the discovery that there is no *prima causa*, that every cause of an effect is in turn the effect of a previous cause and that every author of a fictional character is himself a character in the fiction of a preceding author. Vonnegut's playful claim that "I myself am a work of fiction" and Billy's re-enactment of scenes from Kilgore Trout's *The Big Board* equally attest to this insight, and thus it is small wonder that *Slaughterhouse-Five* constitutes what John Barth dubbed "Another story about a writer writing a story! Another regressus in infinitum!" The narrative game with instances of mediation that can be endlessly multiplied is introduced by the infinitely repeatable song about Yon Yonson and the self-reflexive network of quotations within quotations. These elements are the structural equivalents of the novel's overall message that each answer which man discovers in his painful search for meaning only leads to another question and that consequently not even an eyewitness account of the Dresden massacre can provide this historical event with any objective meaning, but has to be content with a resigned "So it goes."

   The subtitle of *Slaughterhouse-Five* announces that it is "a novel," but its first sentence reads: "All of this happened, more or less." This laconic statement constitutes a disturbing violation of traditional reader expectations and creates considerable ontological insecurity. And the following sentence —"The war parts, anyway, are pretty much true"—only intensifies this insecurity and includes the venerable concept of poetic truth in the bewildering game with fact and fiction. Vonnegut says that as an eye-witness he had thought it would be easy to write his Dresden book, "since all I would have to do would be to report what I had seen," but he admits that this expectation turned out to be completely wrong. Consequently, he discards the mimesis principle as no longer adequate, and his resigned characterizations of his novel as a "lousy little book" and "a failure" exemplify how a fictional context can relativize a factual statement. When the narrative proper begins with "Billy Pilgrim has come unstuck in time," only to thrice qualify this statement by a skeptical "he says," it not only insinuates that Billy exists also outside the text, but the unusual choice of a reporting instead of a narrating tense constitutes another disruption of reader expectations. These strategies are obviously meant to forestall an effect that was long taken for granted but is now unmasked as a momentous misunderstanding: any narrative reconstruction of a historical event cannot but proceed by selection and valuation and is thus by its very definition a sense-making endeavor. Therefore, a traditionally told novel about the destruction of Dresden would be in danger of providing the massacre with a meaning and of unwittingly contributing to a domestication of its horror. And it is this effect which Vonnegut does his very best to prevent, for his novel is meant to convey the opposite message, namely, that "there is nothing intelligent to say about a massacre."

The third strategy that helps to establish the carefully wrought pattern behind the surface disorder is the artful cumulation of repetitions in changing configurations. At first, the dirty limerick and the song about Yon Yonson seem mere digressions, but the latter is integrated into the narrator's discourse when he refers to himself by saying "My name is Yon Yonson [. . .]," and soon the referential texture is so firmly established that a serious reflection on human transitoriness can simply consist of a collage of new and previous references: "*Eheu, fugaces labuntur anni.* My name is Yon Yonson. There was a young man from Stamboul." Gerhard Müller's Germanism "if the accident will," which the author-narrator "like[s] very much" and envisions as the title of a planned story, later turns out to be a centrally important comment on the contingency of human history. The curiously inappropriate comparison of the narrator's alcoholic breath with "mustard gas and roses," which is taken up when he thinks he can smell "mustard gas and roses" through the telephone, achieves thematic significance when Billy experiences the mountains of corpses in Dresden as stinking "like roses and mustard gas" and the smell becomes a metaphorical bracket between narrative present and narrated past, between Vonnegut and Billy Pilgrim. The definition of young soldiers as "foolish virgins" proves literally true for Billy; the ironically misnamed Pope Innocent the Third's praise of the children who go on Crusades is subverted by Roethke's poem and ironically confirmed by Billy's behavior; and the questioning "Poo-tee-weet?" of the birds assumes new meanings when it is taken up in different contexts. These and many other details from the introductory chapter gradually grow into carefully wrought chains of repetitions and variations, which not only provide the inset story with a meaningful texture but also remind the reader that Vonnegut is still haunted by the events which he makes his fictional protagonist go through.

The first chapter, however, not only establishes Vonnegut's innovative narrative strategies, but also thematizes the novel's essential concerns in an oblique way. These concerns are the fraudulent opposition between being and appearance, the ubiquity of human transitoriness and death, and the crucial alternative between either capitulating before life's inherent meaninglessness or attempting to discover and, if necessary, even to invent a meaning for it. With regard to the opposition between appearance and reality, which is already apparent in the uncertain status of Billy's time-travels, Vonnegut contrasts the notion of warfare as embodied by "Frank Sinatra and John Wayne or some of those other glamorous, war-loving, dirty old men" in their mendacious Hollywood movies with his painfully different experience. Thus, he ironically subverts what the mass media disseminate as historical truth and reveals the patriotic discourse about heroism, comradeship and manly self-fulfillment as a variation of what Mackay, more than a hundred years earlier, had unmasked as *Extraordinary Popular Delusions and the Madness of Crowds*. Vonnegut depicts Billy and his fellow soldiers as helpless and disoriented children, and he employs frequent cross-references to the medieval children's crusade in order to debunk with terrible efficiency the widespread macho-images of heroic soldierhood. And since such images originate from the faulty values shared by societies, he once more makes use of the Tralfamadorians' pacifist perspective not only for satirically unmasking the mendacity of patriotic fervor and hero worship as well as the belief in progress and Social Darwinism, but also for bitingly exposing such social institutions as organized Christianity and the American economic system.

Like many modern novels, *Slaughterhouse-Five* is essentially an exploration of the nature of time and death and once again it is the first chapter that thematizes these notions and prepares for Billy's being "spastic in time." From the fact that Vonnegut's wife "always has to know the time" to his resigned remark that it is "always time to go" and to his visit to the World's Fair exhibitions of "the past [. . .] according to the Ford Motor Company and Walt Disney [and] what the future would be like, according to General Motors," and from the necessity of Earthlings "to believe whatever clocks said—and calendars" to Vonnegut's useless "outline" of his novel "on the back of a roll of wallpaper," the first chapter abounds in pertinent references. In the story proper this concern is taken up by Billy Pilgrim, an optician turned metaphysician who prescribes "corrective lenses for Earthling souls," when he proclaims the Tralfamadorian gospel as based on a new perception of time. Thus Vonnegut's musing about "how wide [the present] was, how deep it was, how much was mine to keep," is answered by Billy's assertion that "it is just an illusion we have here on Earth that one moment follows another one." And the concern with human mortality, that makes all art a "dance with death," is not only translated into ironically relevant actions when Billy in his flight from death by hostile bullets performs "involuntary dancing" movements and leaves tracks in the snow that look like "diagrams in a book on ballroom dancing," but it is also triumphantly overcome by the Tralfamadorian concept of death as "just violet light—and a hum," which is experienced only temporarily and resembles the pretense that soldiers are "theoretically dead" in a maneuver.

Once more, then, the unusual structure of the novel, in which the linear succession of a chronologically unfolding plot is replaced by circular spatiality, is revealed as the formal equivalent of its contradictory message. And the structural daredevilry of Vonnegut's experiment becomes obvious when one compares the traditional outline for his book with a beginning, a middle, and an end, which he discards as useless, with the Tralfamadorian novels, in which a surprised Billy finds "no beginning, no middle, no end, no suspense, no moral, no causes, no effects" but simply "the depths of many marvelous moments seen all at one time." Of course, the time-bound nature of human language prevents a narrative that is just an atemporal "clump of symbols," but within the given limits Vonnegut successfully discards the logical succession of beginning, middle, and end, does away with suspense by not only quoting the final line of his novel at its very beginning but by also prematurely disclosing that "the climax of the book will be the execution of poor old Edgar Derby," disrupts any cause-and-effect sequence through the radical fragmentation of his fable, and refuses to provide his tale with a clearly recognizable moral. Thus, he turns his idiosyncratic tale into "a Duty-Dance with Death" (subtitle) and, in the process, elevates his fictional evocation of the Dresden firestorm into a philosophical inquiry into the conditions of human existence.

Both the ubiquitous discrepancy between appearance and reality and the ineluctability of human transitoriness point to the central concern of *Slaughterhouse-Five*, namely, the desperate quest for the meaning of a life that permits events as gruesome as the Dresden massacre. And this concern, too, is multiply thematized in the introductory chapter. The taxidriver's formulation "if the accident will" aptly diagnoses the contingency of human existence, and the quotations from Céline and Roethke point to modern literature's obsession with the transitoriness of life. Harrison Starr's claim that "there would always be wars" highlights the impotence of reason, and Edgar Derby's execution illustrates the unbearable injustice of human systems of order. The ludicrous answer of the Air Force that details about the bombing of Dresden are "top secret still" is a frightening exercise in illogicality, and Vonnegut's anthropological insight "that there was absolutely no difference between anybody" is the very apogee of absurdity. In the story proper the quest for meaning is continued on the level of the surface action by repeated questions that range form Billy's bewildered "Why me?" and the title of the propagandistic pamphlet "Why We Fight" to an American POW's astonished "Why me?" and the "Why?" of Billy's dream about giraffes. But at the same time such questions are rejected as meaningless by the Tralfamadorians, who consider "free will" an illusion, smile about Earthlings as "the great explainers, explaining why this event is structured as it is, telling how other events may be achieved or avoided, " and flatly insist that "there is no why. " But in spite of the many similarities between Vonnegut and his protagonist, there is an easily overlooked but decisive difference. Implementing Vonnegut's admission that his novel has no real characters because they are all "so sick and so much the listless playthings of enormous forces," Billy comes to the insight that "*everything* is all right, and everybody has to do exactly what he does" and thus abandons the concepts of free will and individual responsibility in favor of a resigned fatalism. Vonnegut, however, draws a totally different conclusion from his Dresden experience, because he educates his sons to be pacifists, constantly makes moral judgments, and is certainly "not overjoyed" by the Tralfamadorian teachings. The very facts that he manages to write *Slaughterhouse-Five*, that, like Lot's wife, he is "so human" that he looks back, and that he exhorts his readers to "listen" to a tale which he admits to be "a failure" testify to the difference between an actively protesting Vonnegut and his fatalistic protagonist and furnish the novel with an unresolved philosophical tension that confronts its readers with the task of re-examining their own positions and wresting their individual meaning from an incomprehensible world.

This does not mean, however, that *Slaughterhouse-Five* indulges in cynical relativism. On the contrary, it keeps competing views of what happened in Dresden and why in a precarious and irritating balance by offering mutually incompatible explanations. In his "Address to the American Physical Society" (1969) Vonnegut says in no uncertain terms that "the Second World War was a war against pure evil. [. . .] Nothing was too horrible to do to any enemy that vile," but in his introduction to a new edition of *Mother Night* he frankly admits that "if I'd been born in Germany, I suppose I would have been a Nazi." It is this unresolved tension that makes Billy, who is wracked by sudden crying fits, weep for both the guilt of the Allied perpetrators and for the guilt of the German victims who provoked the bombardment and that prevents the novel from offering some pat moral by accusing anyone in particular. Instead it evokes a spectrum of reactions that ranges from Billy's fatalistic notion that "everybody has to do exactly what he does" and the disinterested Tralfamadorian perspective that "those who die are meant to die, that corpses are improvements" to the narrator's outrage at the fact that humans have repeated the same cruelties from the medieval Crusades through the destruction of Dresden to the war in Vietnam. In his influential novel *Cat's Cradle*, that became a cult book of the youthful counterculture of the sixties, Vonnegut makes his self-styled social messiah Bokonon resignedly observe "History! Read it and weep!," and it is this very desperation about man's inability to learn that sets the tone of *Slaughterhouse-Five*.

In a 1973 interview Vonnegut admits his inability to face the gory details of the Dresden massacre, when he says that

> there was a complete blank where the bombing of Dresden took place, because I don't remember. And I looked up several

of my war buddies and they didn't remember, either. They didn't want to talk about it. There was a complete forgetting of what it was like. There were all kinds of information surrounding the event, but as far as my memory bank was concerned, the center had been pulled right out of the story.

Of course, it is Vonnegut's survivor's guilt and his need to suppress the unbearable horror that offer biographical reasons for the fact that the thematic center of his novel is endlessly circumnavigated but never fully encountered and that only a few gory details such as the digging up of rotting bodies from "hundreds of corpse mines" or the cremation of the dead "with flamethrowers" are briefly referred to. But Vonnegut makes an epistemological virtue of this psychological necessity by going after a more inclusive target, namely the delusion of war in general. At all times, wars have cruelly deprived children of their childhood, destroyed priceless cultural values, and wiped out innocent lives, and thus it makes perfect sense that in his "anti-war book" the Dresden firestorm is seen as just another instance in the endless sequence of human brutality from Sodom and Gomorrha through the medieval Crusades to the jungle war in Vietnam. Moreover, Vonnegut tells his story at a time about which he coolly observes:

> Robert Kennedy, [. . .], was shot two nights ago. He died last night. So it goes.
> Martin Luther King was shot a month ago. He died, too. So it goes.
> And every day my government gives me a count of corpses created by military science in Vietnam. So it goes.

An audience that is increasingly immunized against atrocities by being exposed by the mass media to its daily allowance of mutilated corpses can hardly be roused by yet another novel with realistic details about the horrors of war, and this is why Vonnegut, like Joseph Heller in his *Catch-22*, has to resort to other strategies. His painfully understated "anti-war book" abandons all attempts at mimetic recreation and instead conveys its outrage about the constant continuation of atrocities by showing that there is no appropriate response to the Dresden massacre. Vonnegut's seemingly unconcerned attitude is easily recognizable as a defense mechanism, and his use of science-fiction strategies, of which he aptly says they serve the same function as "the clowns in Shakespeare," signals not a lack of taste but a desperate attempt at coping with the irrationality of mass extermination and at effecting what De Quincey in his essay about the porter scene in *Macbeth* calls 'the reflux of the human upon the fiendish.' His narrative reduction of a massive historical event to the multiple-refracted interplay between a traumatized narrator who needs to keep his experience at bay, and a helpless protagonist who hardly understands what is happening to him, turns out to be a highly successful way of translating a historical atrocity, which transcends all human imagination, into the realm of individual empathy and of thus confronting the puzzled reader with the task of co-authoring the shocking meaning of a tale which is an accomplished example of how a historical event can be imaginatively storified by means of advanced metafictional strategies.

PHILIP WATTS

Rewriting History: Céline and Kurt Vonnegut

Midway through his 1975 introduction to a paperback edition of Céline's
last three novels—*Castle to Castle*, *North*, and *Rigadoon*—Kurt Vonnegut
confesses: "I get a splitting headache every time I try to write about Céline.
I have one now. I never have headaches at any other time." Through this
quip Vonnegut points to a process of identification with Céline that begins
on the biographical level—the two writers have the same "unusual head" and
share similar literary concerns. But his headache is also a symptom of the
problematic nature of Vonnegut's reception of Céline, for what comes out of
the relation between these two authors is not only the traditional issue of
literary influence, but also the problem of historical revisionism and
ideological transmission. Vonnegut's 1969 account of the destruction of
Dresden, *Slaughterhouse-Five*, is to a great extent a rewriting of the war
sequences in Céline's 1932 *Voyage au bout de la nuit*. As his 1975 essay makes
clear, however, Vonnegut may have turned to Céline not only for his
innovative style, but also because of his proximity to fascist politics after
1936. In exploring an issue that had been bracketed by Céline's earlier
American readers, Vonnegut also comes dangerously close to reproducing
Céline's attempts in his trilogy to rewrite the history of World War II in
terms that were more compatible with his wartime politics.

When Vonnegut wrote this eight-page introductory essay, he was at the

From *The South Atlantic Quarterly* Vol. 93 no. 2 (Spring 1994). © 1994 by Duke University Press.

height of his national popularity. Generally recognized as one of the voices of the emerging counterculture, he had just published the best-selling *Breakfast of Champions* and commanded imposing sums on the college lecture circuit. From the opening paragraphs of his introduction, Vonnegut acknowledges that he owes at least part of his success to Céline; he states that in fact "every writer is in his debt." Perhaps because he has had such success in the marketplace, Vonnegut ties literary influence to the notion of debt, and his essay exploits a metaphoric potential already at work in the discourse on literature. We speak, after all, of an author's legacy, of his gift, of his heirs, of his contribution to a literary tradition, of various writers' indebtedness to their precursors, and of the homage writers pay to one another as if the very idea of cultural transmission depended upon a form of economic exchange. But if the terminology of economics seems to be present whenever we begin to speak of literary influence, for Vonnegut it should not be read as merely metaphoric. Céline's presence is literally a present, a gift that Vonnegut will treat as a debt.

In his short introductory piece, Vonnegut makes it clear that his debt stems from his discovery of Céline's work during the period when he was writing *Slaughterhouse-Five*. Vonnegut relates his feelings upon reading *Journey to the End of the Night* for the first time: "The book penetrated my bones, anyway, if not my mind. And I only now understand what I took from Céline and put into the novel I was writing at the time, which was called *Slaughterhouse-Five*." I will return to the specific links between *Journey to the End of the Night* and Vonnegut's novel, but first I want to emphasize that his reading of Céline inspired Vonnegut to complete the war novel he had been trying to write for some twenty-five years, a novel that not only secured his place in American letters but became his first commercial success and generated a lucrative movie contract with a Hollywood studio. Vonnegut is acutely aware that his success in the American literary marketplace was due, at least in part, to the gift of a French author who ended his life in relative poverty, who used the language of impoverished "guttersnipes," and whose sales in America remain low. Vonnegut not only acknowledges his debt to Céline, but his use of the reimbursement metaphor determines the entire introductory essay. Although it is unclear whether Vonnegut played a part in getting Céline's postwar novels translated and distributed, his introduction to a trade paperback edition of the works may have been a way to initiate the repayment process. After all, Vonnegut began his own career by publishing his novels as paperback originals, a move that was predicated on the desire for increased sales and that tied Vonnegut inextricably to popular science fiction and other pulp fiction genres. In any case, Vonnegut defines Céline's place in the canon of modern literature by comparing him to Hemingway and suggesting that maybe Céline, too, should have been awarded the Nobel Prize. Vonnegut's essay is not only a panegyric on Céline's literary merits, but also an attempt to bolster the market for his works.

There is, however, another aspect to this reimbursement motif that does not figure in the Penguin edition at all, but is made explicit in the title Vonnegut tacked onto the piece when he reprinted it in *Palm Sunday*, his 1981 autobiographical collage. Here, the essay bears the title, "A Nazi Sympathizer Defended at Some Cost." Six years after the original publication of the essay, Vonnegut was still caught in the web of debt and repayment, of inheritance and reimbursement. He was not only indebted to Céline for his success, but chose to honor that debt through what he considered a pro bono defense. Vonnegut may have been paid for writing the introduction to the Penguin edition, but he included it in his autobiographical collection, as he says, "with no financial gain in prospect." Furthermore, Vonnegut insists that the essay could harm his reputation, which is firmly anchored in a liberal, humanist, pacifist tradition—"many people will believe that I share many of [Céline's] authentically vile opinions."

Although Vonnegut doesn't intend to justify Céline's anti-Semitism, the position he adopts forces him to confront the French author's politics. He is quick to set up a clear distinction between the diatribes of the pamphlets and the novels, from which Vonnegut claims, Céline's "cracked politics" are "virtually exclude[d]." Vonnegut is here repeating Céline's own statements made after the war—that his novels were stylistic events, purged of all political ideology, a position that Céline first adopted during his 1950 trial for collaboration. Of Céline's pamphlets, Vonnegut writes: "His words are contemptible to anyone who has suffered from anti-Semitism." At the same time, however, Vonnegut finds what he calls "a twisted sort of honor in [Céline's] declining to offer excuses of any kind." In sticking by his opinions, Vonnegut seems to be saying, Céline was being honorable. This is the point in his essay where Vonnegut complains of a headache, as if it were a symptom, a physical manifestation, of the untenability of this defense. Ultimately, Vonnegut resorts to the defense that isn't one: in attempting to explain Céline's hatred, Vonnegut can say only that he has "heard no explanation for this other than" that Céline "was partly insane." Vonnegut's introduction, then, provides Céline with an elaborate defense based on the insanity plea. It is as if, in Vonnegut's mind, Céline could be read by the American public only after he had been acquitted of his intellectual crimes. But in defending Céline, Vonnegut also evades the fact that Céline's novels, from *Féerie pour une autre fois* to *Rigadoon*, can be read as stylized attempts to rewrite the war in relation to the terms of his own defense. The real difficulty in reading Céline comes from the fact that any attempt to rehabilitate the novels reproduces precisely the arguments Céline himself had used in justifying his political positions.

Still, even if Vonnegut attempts to exorcise Céline's "cracked politics" from the later novels, he is nonetheless one of the few American writers to have confronted this political aspect of Céline, an aspect that, because the pamphlets haven't been translated, hasn't undergone the process of cultural transmission. Whereas Allen Ginsberg praised Céline for incorporating "aural speech patterns" into his prose and read him as a great vilifier, Vonnegut ties this use of the vernacular to a "privileged" perspective on historical events. If Vonnegut is in Céline's debt, it is not because of the "three dot" style, a technique that Vonnegut claims can be imitated only by gossip columnists ("They like its looks," he writes, perhaps referring to Herb Caen of the *San Francisco Chronicle*), but because Céline, in Vonnegut's view, was the first modern writer to use a vernacular in the representation of historical events. This stylistic innovation by Céline produced what Vonnegut calls the "finest novels we have of the total collapse of Western civilization in two world wars, as witnessed by hideously vulnerable common men and women." Vonnegut is thus promoting an assessment of Céline as not just a stylistic innovator, but also a war novelist who lived through and recorded two cataclysmic historical events. Céline becomes Vonnegut's model for rewriting history, but it is precisely through this rewriting that the problem of "cracked politics" reappears.

While Vonnegut seems to present a politics-free Céline to the U.S. reading public, it is possible nonetheless that he was attracted to Céline *because* rather than *despite* his Nazi sympathies. Vonnegut's identification with Céline may take place at the level of his politics. Although it is often parodic, often to the second degree, Vonnegut's fiction constantly returns to an attraction to fascism, a tendency identified by Saul Friedländer in other texts of the same period that exhibit a desire not so much to excuse as to understand and perhaps also to exorcise, to purge the guilt associated with fascist atrocities. One of Vonnegut's early novels, *Mother Night*, is presented as the confessions of Howard W. Campbell, Jr., an American Nazi and fascist propagandist who writes his autobiography while awaiting trial for war crimes in an Israeli jail (his cell is next to Eichmann's). Vonnegut has continued to ask himself what it means to be a German-American after World War II, even inscribing his own family fictionally in historical events of the war. In a 1980 lecture on filial ties delivered to the Mental Health Association of New Jersey, he told the story of an imaginary psychiatrist named "Colonel Vonnegut," who "cured" the S.S. staff at Auschwitz so they could keep on killing. And in his 1982 novel *Deadeye Dick*, the narrator's father befriends the young Hitler in prewar Vienna, saves his life by buying one of his paintings, and flies a swastika flag outside the family home in Midland City, Ohio. Vonnegut uses German fascism to reflect upon the values of contemporary American society, a society that he at once admires and distrusts. At the same time, however, these representations of "Nazi sympathizers" dangerously scramble notions of guilt and innocence and come close to being exculpatory. Vonnegut's novels, like his introduction to Céline's, are also defendants' insanity pleas, and his characters are all afflicted with the same type of "insanity" attributed to Céline, a madness in which the attraction to an ideology of hate paradoxically verges on moral purity. Vonnegut's attempt to launch Céline's last works must thus be read not only as a defense of the French writer, but also as an effort to legitimize some of Vonnegut's own concerns about politics, anti-Semitism, and World War II.

   If in his 1975 essay Vonnegut reflects upon his use of Céline, his 1969 war novel, *Slaughterhouse-Five*, can be read at least partly in relation to Céline's 1932 *Voyage au bout de la nuit*. While linked to other contexts— science fiction, suburban satire, and 1960s counterculture—*Slaughterhouse-Five* depends nonetheless on the opening sections of Céline's first novel for both its tone and its representation of war. In the first few pages Vonnegut tells us that, while awaiting a flight to Germany, he began to read Erika Ostrovsky's 1967 study, *Céline and His Vision*. A passage by Céline, lifted from Ostrovsky's work, sets the mood for the rest of Vonnegut's novel: "No art is possible without a dance with death . . . The truth is death . . . I've fought nicely against it as long as I could . . . danced with it, festooned it, waltzed it around." Céline's presence as a writer who directly confronted death is thus inscribed at the beginning of Vonnegut's novel. Even the book's first page echoes this voice since one of the alternate titles of *Slaughterhouse-Five* is "A Duty-Dance with Death." Both authors witnessed the destructive force of war and placed this wartime experience at the center of their literary endeavors. What Vonnegut inherits from Céline is a terminology of spectacle with which to represent and ultimately to condemn the horrors of war, as well as a protagonist who remains uncomprehending when faced with this destruction.

   Vonnegut's alter-title on the inseparability of death and dance may have been culled from Ostrovsky's study, but there can be little doubt that he had already found this deathly aesthetic in Céline's representations of World War I. In the opening chapters of *Journey to the End of the Night*, for example, Céline applies the vocabulary of spectacle to his representations of the battlefield. After the gruesome death of the colonel, Bardamu compares him to a vaudevillian:

I thought again of the colonel and how fine the fellow looked, with his cuirass and his helmet and his mustaches. Put him on at a music hall, walking about among the bullets and shells as I had seen him, and the turn would have filled the Alhambra those days. He'd have wiped the floor with Fragson herself, though at the time I'm speaking of she was tremendously popular.

With these references to the Alhambra, a famous music hall before the war, and to Fragson, one of the most popular music hall singers of the time, Céline begins transforming reality into spectacle. A little later, Bardamu compares himself to a "spectator" watching villages burn, which he likens to a "fair ground" and a "pretty sight." These are just a few examples of a sign system that is ubiquitous in Céline's novels, a commingling of theatrical and martial terminology that Céline would more fully exploit later in his World War II novels.

In *Slaughterhouse-Five*, the reader is also confronted with wartime spectacles and with war as spectacle. Arriving at a prison camp in Germany, Billy Pilgrim and the other American soldiers are entertained by British prisoners who stage their own version of *Cinderella*. This show is echoed in the narrative by the characters' transforming themselves into actors. As the novel progresses, Billy Pilgrim slowly changes into costume until, just before the bombing, he is clad in a blue toga and silver slippers. The residents of Dresden who get their first look at American soldiers then are amazed at the merry sight of "these hundred ridiculous creatures," a description that Vonnegut concludes: "Here were more crippled human beings, more fools like themselves. Here was light opera." And within this operatic troupe/military troop, "Billy Pilgrim was the star." Later still, moments after the destruction of Dresden by Allied bombs, the four soldiers assigned to guard the American prisoners are described as open-mouthed, looking "like a silent film of a barbershop quartet."

Although the use of theatrical terminology in a literary text is not unusual, there are certain peculiarities that tie Vonnegut's spectacle to Céline's. The spectacles in both works reveal a nostalgia for somewhat outdated musical forms. In an American context, the barbershop quartet plays the same role as the Alhambra music hall does in the French setting. Both represent a style that is popular, vernacular, somewhat naive, and hopelessly passé. Vonnegut developed this type of allusion in later novels, drawing on the films of Laurel and Hardy for his 1976 novel, *Slapstick*, and speaking of the "music" of artillery shells in *Hocus Pocus*, published in 1990. The theatrical terminology never obscures the historical referent, however.

In *Slaughterhouse-Five*, as in *Journey to the End of the Night*, the spectacular vocabulary facilitates the transition from lived experience to literary text and functions, paradoxically, as a central component in the author's quest to rewrite history. Not only do both authors use this theatricality to satirize military discipline, but Vonnegut's work, like Céline's, asserts its fictionality in order to confront and contradict what each author sees as the official discourse of history. Whereas *Journey to the End of the Night* destabilizes the discourse of patriotism and nationalist authority, Vonnegut's spectacular text directly confronts a central aspect of American cultural history: the epic war movie. In the opening passages of *Slaughterhouse-Five* the author sets up this confrontation when he promises a friend that he will never write a novel that might be turned into a movie starring John Wayne or Frank Sinatra. Vonnegut is offering his pacifist spectacle of the war in opposition to such pro-war spectacles as *The Longest Day*. It is an irony of American cultural production that *Slaughterhouse-Five* was turned into a Hollywood movie only a few years after its publication.

The second aspect of Céline's legacy to Vonnegut is the creation of a wide-eyed, candid protagonist. Vonnegut tells us that after reading *Journey to the End of the Night*, he felt compelled to write the phrase "so it goes" each time someone, or something, died. Here is how Vonnegut explains the use of this phrase:

> It was a clumsy way of saying what Céline managed to imply so much more naturally in everything he wrote, in effect: "Death and suffering can't matter nearly as much as I think they do. Since they are so common, my taking them seriously must mean that I am insane. I must try to be saner."

This statement, loaded with irony, must be read as implying the contrary of what it proposes. Rather than expressing resignation in the face of death, *Slaughterhouse-Five* constantly expresses horror at the atrocity of war, and we quickly realize that if Vonnegut pleads insanity, as he did for Céline, it is only because he feels so out of touch with a society that would permit the massive annihilation seen during wartime. After the liminary chapter, *Slaughterhouse-Five* is told from the perspective of Billy Pilgrim, a successful suburban optometrist in the 1960s and a somewhat bemused private in the U.S. Army during World War II. Billy Pilgrim's fundamental characteristic is his naive, candid outlook as he witnesses the destruction of Dresden. It is this view of war, conveyed by a passive, alienated, and candid narrator that Vonnegut "takes" from Céline.

There is little doubt that Céline's use of invective is unsurpassed in twentieth-century literature. Still, countering the accumulation of diatribe and hyperbole is Céline's use of understatement, usually channeled through the voice of a somewhat confused narrator. In *Journey to the End of the Night*, Bardamu's candid worldview is perhaps best demonstrated by the famous phrase "[one] is as innocent of Horror as one is of sex," and much of the novel is constructed around Bardamu's loss of innocence. Directly echoing Céline's claims about the innocence of the young troops, Vonnegut writes: "We *had* been foolish virgins in the war right at the end of childhood." (Vonnegut's "virgins" was, as it turns out, much closer to the term Céline had originally used: "puceau.") In one of the first scenes of *Journey to the End of the Night*, Bardamu realizes that two German soldiers are shooting at him and aiming to kill. Rather than feeling fright or anger, Bardamu's reaction is incomprehension: "The colonel perhaps knew why those two fellows were firing and the Germans maybe knew it too; but as for me, quite frankly, I didn't at all." A little later he exclaims: "I felt somehow I ought to be polite to the Germans." Thirty years later, Billy Pilgrim reacted to a German sniper in the same way Bardamu had: "Billy stood there politely, giving the marksman another chance. It was his addled understanding of the rules of warfare that the marksman *should* be given a second chance." And where Céline had described enemy bullets as "swarm[ing] . . . wasps," Vonnegut called them "lethal bee[s]," changing the species but not the genus of the referent.

One character in *Slaughterhouse-Five* not only understands but actually enjoys the madness of war: Roland Weary, an antitank gunner from Pittsburgh whose specialty and avocation is torture. If Bardamu was the model for Billy Pilgrim, Roland Weary's model was perhaps Lieutenant Saint-Engence, the officer in *Journey to the End of the Night* who delights in showing his blood-caked sword to his comrades. Weary spends most of the war quizzing Billy Pilgrim on the worst forms of torture and execution, asking questions that the young soldier can never answer. When, for example, Roland Weary explains the use of a bayonet's "blood gutter," Billy's innocence recalls Bardamu's response on seeing the lieutenant's weapon: " . . . he held out his sabre for them to see. There was indeed some dried blood on it, which filled the little groove made for that purpose." The emphasis on the troops' innocence, their awkward politeness, and the correspondences between secondary characters all mark the tight textual links between the two works. They share an ideological stance as well, for in *Slaughterhouse-Five*, as in *Journey to the End of the Night*, the main character's incomprehension before these horrors permits the author to enlist the reader's sympathy in his acerbic condemnation of war.

Vonnegut's reception of Céline is thus at once stylistic and political in the sense that *Slaughterhouse-Five* incorporates a denunciation of war. But there is another side to the ideology at work in Vonnegut's novel that is troubling, to say the least, and that has to do with his representation of the destruction of Dresden, the novel's real story. Vonnegut was writing against what he considered the official history of World War II, but in doing so he launched his work down the slippery slope of historical revisionism, forcing us to reconsider both *Slaughterhouse-Five* and the nature of his reception of Céline.

When Billy Pilgrim, in his 1960s incarnation, is hospitalized, he must share a room with a rather loud, self-assured "retired brigadier general in the Air Force Reserve" named Bertrand Copeland Rumfoord, professor of history at Harvard and author of the twenty-seven volume *Official History of the Army Air Force in World War Two*, in which, predictably, there is "almost nothing . . . about the Dresden raid." A few pages later, Professor Rumfoord reads Ira C. Eaker's introduction to an actual study by David Irving entitled *The Destruction of Dresden*, in which Eaker reiterates the reasons why bombing the German city was necessary. In his last scene Rumfoord defends the bombings by simply stating: "It *had* to be done." There is little doubt that both Rumfoord, a fictional Harvard historian, and Eaker, a real Air Force general, express the orthodox government and academic view of the war. To counter this history, Billy Pilgrim, in a voice tremulous to the point of being inaudible, can only say, "I was there."

In this presentation of official history there is a subtle twisting of historiography on Vonnegut's part. Although Rumfoord is a fictional creation, there is in fact a German historian named Hans Rumpf, whose study, *The Bombing of Germany*, strongly condemns the Allied air raids. And although Ira C. Eaker's introduction to Irving's work justifies the Dresden bombings, Irving himself ultimately denounces the Allied action. Both Rumpf and Irving share Vonnegut's view, but his silence about the content of their studies suggests a desire to be the lone voice of a counter-history that would both represent and condemn the massive destruction of Dresden. Because it remains vernacular and slightly naive, the novel seems to be the only genre through which Vonnegut could present what he had attributed to Céline: a history of the "total collapse of Western civilization . . . as witnessed by hideously vulnerable common women and men." And just as Céline's 1932 novel has been read not only as an indictment of World War I, but also as a pacifist manifesto against what Céline saw as the mounting belligerence in France in the 1930s, Vonnegut's novel can be read as an allegory condemning the American air raids launched against North Vietnam in the late 1960s.

There is, however, a second, more troubling aspect to what Vonnegut conceptualizes as his struggle against an official silence on the bombing raids. The 1969 novel raises questions that Vonnegut would return to in his 1975 essay, questions of guilt and responsibility concerning the war. The opening chapter of *Slaughterhouse-Five* relates how, as a graduate student in Chicago, Vonnegut once told a professor, who "was a member of a thing called the Committee for Social Thought," that he was writing a book on the Dresden air raids. The professor responded by invoking the torture and extermination of Jews in the Nazi concentration camps, causing Vonnegut to reply, "I know, I know. I *know*." Vonnegut's response remains elliptical, but it can be read as the expression of his exasperation at having to hear, once again, about the horror of the death camps. As Vonnegut vents his frustration at not being able to write about his experience, the text suggests a systematic comparison between the destruction of Dresden, on the one hand, and the Holocaust, on the other. This comparison is implicit in the 1975 essay, where Vonnegut writes: "As the war was ending [Céline] headed for the center of the holocaust—Berlin." The reference is to the bombing of Berlin, but we cannot read the term "holocaust" without suspecting that in his defense of Céline Vonnegut is attempting to replace one horror with another, particularly since he places the anti-Semite rather than the Jew at the center of this "holocaust." Although Vonnegut makes a few references to Nazi extermination camps in *Slaughterhouse-Five*, the bombing of Germany, rather than the German Holocaust, becomes for him the massacre that is situated beyond the bounds of representation. It is as if, in Vonnegut's work, the Holocaust is silenced so that the fire-bombing of Dresden may be heard. This rhetoric of substitution leads Vonnegut to call the bombing "the greatest massacre in European history."

What is most disturbing about this type of comparison is that it relies upon a system of false analogies, which has become one of the principal rhetorical tools of negationists, whose goal is to deny the fact of the Holocaust. Drawing this type of analogy inevitable leads to what Alain Finkielkraut has called "lying two times"—once about the bombings and a second time about the death camps—the first step in the negationists' falsification of history. One of the most notorious among these negationists is David Irving, whom Vonnegut cites and whose book about the bombing of Dresden was followed by claims that there were no gas chambers at Auschwitz, a statement as outrageous as it is hateful. I do not want to be understood as accusing Vonnegut of being a negationist, but the type of comparison presented in *Slaughterhouse-Five* reiterates the arguments used to defend Nazi war criminals at the end of World War II. Allied air raids on Germany and Japan were cited to excuse the atrocities committed by the

Nazis in the extermination camps. If Vonnegut didn't learn this rhetoric of comparison from Céline—in 1969 Vonnegut had probably read only *Journey to the End of the Night*—*Slaughterhouse-Five* nevertheless foreshadows both Céline's last novels, and their implicit comparison between the death camps and the bombing raids on Germany, and Vonnegut's own need to defend a "Nazi sympathizer."

Analyzing Céline's presence in Vonnegut's work forces us beyond the traditional boundaries of the source study and the tracing of literary influence. In processing the intertextual links between these two authors it is necessary to consider not only the similarities of style, lexicon, and imagery, but also the transmission of ideologies. Vonnegut's reception of Céline seems most pronounced when it is furthest from literary concerns, and it was perhaps his discovery of the nature of this reception that made Vonnegut so anxious to settle his debt to Céline.

LAWRENCE R. BROER

Images of the Shaman in the Works of Kurt Vonnegut

George Bernard Shaw accounted for the savage unreasonableness of mankind by suggesting that some alien world was using the earth as its insane asylum, dropping lunatics off at regular intervals. For such writers as John Barth, Joseph Heller, Thomas Pynchon and Kurt Vonnegut, Shaw's observation of madness at the center of human affairs becomes a disturbingly literal estimate of the human situation in the latter half of the twentieth century. The times are no longer out of joint; they are unimaginable—an ongoing nightmare of violence and unpredictability in which the writer's conception of his world changes from that of Matthew Arnold's "battleground" in "Dover Beach" to the lunatic asylum of Ken Kesey's *One Flew Over the Cuckoo's Nest*, Beckett's *Watt*, or Vonnegut's *God Bless You, Mr. Rosewater*. Responding to the recent writers' obsession with warpedness in what he calls "the literature of 'Extremis,'" Kurt Vonnegut explains, "we all respond with a sort of shriek to the ghastliness of news today . . . It is typical of people who have a gruesome history, who have seen many invasions, a large number of dead people, and many executions."

While these "shrieks" of madness in contemporary fiction occur with important variations, two extremes persist: writers such as Beckett, Donleavy, Barth and Heller, whose bitterness leads to depressing or dispiriting fictions, and writers such as John Gardner, Norman Mailer,

From *Dionysus in Literature: Essays on Literary Madness*, edited by Branimir M. Rieger. © 1994 by Bowling Green State University Popular Press.

Bernard Malamud and Kurt Vonnegut, whose despair is balanced by an optimistic faith in the possibility of change or renewal. The former writers create characters incapable of ordering or coping with contemporary experience, "agitated spirits," as Saul Bellow's Mr. Sammler calls them, "casting themselves into chaos," while the latter seek to restore order and purpose through the affirmation of old values or the creation of new ones. I speak, of course, of polarities which represent reactions to a radical age whose norm is to breed such extremes. Tags such as "affirmative" or "negative" should be used guardedly. Personal sympathies may determine what one finds bracing or dispiriting, and the choice of our best writers to affirm or to deny is not always as clear-cut, as categorical, for instance, as John Gardner would have us believe.

Though hardly unique in reading Vonnegut as a pessimistic writer, Gardner has been more vociferous than most in accusing Vonnegut of "cold-heartedness and trivial-mindedness." Confusing the withdrawal of Vonnegut's often dazed and pliant hero into narcissistic fantasies and escapist daydreams with an absence of moral commitment on the author's part, Gardner claims that "Vonnegut's moral energy is forever flagging, his fight forever turning slapstick." In this same vein, Kalidas Misra sees Vonnegut's vision as so dark, his characters so powerless, she uses *Slaughterhouse-Five* to describe a shift in the modern war novel from "hope to final despair." Critics from David Goldsmith to Josephine Hendin have argued that the philosophic determinism of Tralfamadore in *Slaughterhouse-Five* represents Vonnegut's own sense of the futility of the human condition. It is the wisdom of Tralfamadore, they say, based upon the belief that human events are inevitably structured to be the way they are and hence do not lend themselves to warnings or explanations, that allows Billy Pilgrim and the author to adjust to their traumatic memories of Dresden.

It is usually these same critics who, seeing Vonnegut as a "facile fatalist," fail to understand the psychological function of Vonnegut's exotic settings and imaginary worlds, associating such fantasy creations as Tralfamadore, Titan, Mars, San Lorenzo or Shangri-la with frivolity and superficiality. The fact is that these escapist worlds warn against rather than affirm fatalist sophistries. Such mirror reflections of our own planet enforce Vonnegut's position that the insane world of soulless materialistic lusts for fame and money, of suicidal wars and self-serving religions, that we presently inhabit is a world of our own lunatic invention. The Tralfamadorian view of reality is the very antithesis of Vonnegut's position that artists should be treasured as alarm systems—specialized cells for giving warning to the body politic. The Tralfamadorians eventually blow up the universe while experimenting with new fuels for their flying saucers. They do not improve

Billy's vision; Billy's conversion to Tralfamadorian fatalism OR FATAL DREAM ("Tralfamadore" by anagram), ensures his schizophrenic descent into madness.

John Irving provides valuable counterpoint to the argument by Hendin, Roger Sale, Jack Richardson, John Gardner, et al., that Vonnegut infects his readers with despair and world weariness. Irving agrees that Vonnegut "hurts" us with visions of a ruined planet, evaporated sunny dreams. But Vonnegut's "bleak impoliteness" provokes us to be more thoughtful, creative and kind. Doris Lessing, too, reminds us that Vonnegut explores "the ambiguities of complicity," which causes the reader to think carefully about degrees of responsibility for violence and injustice.

The irony of viewing Vonnegut as a writer of "pessimistic" or "defeatist" novels is that no writer has been more self-conscious in serving his society as a "Shaman," a kind of spiritual medicine man whose function is to expose these various forms of societal madness—dispelling the evil spirits of irresponsible mechanization and aggression while encouraging reflectiveness and the will to positive social change. It is this almost mystical vision of himself as spiritual medium and healer that Vonnegut intends by calling himself a "canary bird in the coal mine"—one who provides spiritual illumination, offering us warnings about the dehumanized future not as it must necessarily be, but as it surely would become if based on the runaway technology of the present. In his novel *Bluebeard*, Vonnegut's artist-protagonist Rabo Karabekian describes his part in "a peculiar membership" with ancient historical roots—people telling stories around a campfire at night or painting pictures on the walls of caves. Its purpose is to cheer people up, inspire fellowship and open up minds that would go on exactly as before "no matter how painful, unrealistic, unjust, ludicrous, or downright dumb . . . life may be." The historical role of Vonnegut's artist-Shaman is described by Mircea Eliade as someone proficient in speculative thought—a singer, poet, musician, diviner, priest and doctor—preserver of oral traditions in literature and of ancient legends.

Both roles—Shaman and canary bird—meet Vonnegut's major criterion for himself as artist—that writers are and biologically have to be agents of change, specialized cells in the social organism. Functioning as the projective imagination of the Life Force, Vonnegut, particularly in his later novels, shapes us a more benign and creative future—one in which human beings feel their common humanity at a deep and emotional level of being. Such a future community would have kindness, awareness, mercy, fairness, charity and mutual respect at its core, symbolized by gentle people sharing a common bowl. It is on behalf of this saner world that Vonnegut directs his satirical missiles, warning us with visions of apocalyptic fury in novels from *The Sirens of Titan* to *Galápagos* that we are a doomed species unless we learn to replace lunatic aggression and cruelty with gentleness and restraint.

In fairness, those critics who see Vonnegut as a fatalist are partially right. It seems that for a long while the author's fictional voice is dualistic—"split . . . right up the middle" (as is said of Paul Proteus in *Player Piano*) into a self that affirms and a self that denies. It is the fierce combat of these warring identities, referred to by Freud in *Beyond the Pleasure Principle* as a battle between the forces of Eros, the life instinct, and Thanatos, the death instinct, which the tormented Howard Campbell in *Mother Night* calls "schizophrenic," and whose attempts at resolution constitute the psychoanalytic plot central to each of Vonnegut's novels and to his work as a whole. Wavering conviction as to the possibility of human progress once caused Vonnegut to remark that "Shaw's optimism in *Back to Methuselah* was science fiction enough for me." Vonnegut commented that he suffered from "Hunter Thompson disease"—the affliction of "all those who feel that Americans can be as easily led to beauty as to ugliness, to truth as to public relations, to joy as to bitterness . . . I don't have it this morning. It comes and it goes." So come and go the efforts of Vonnegut's early protagonists, Paul Proteus, Malachi Constant, Howard Campbell, Jonah and Eliot Rosewater to overcome that fear, cynicism and will-lessness which impedes the spiritual growth of Vonnegut's prospective Shaman-hero. Significantly, Eliade observes that the Shaman—the primitive magician, the medicine man—is above all one who has successfully cured himself. Through his own psychodrama he knows the mechanism, the theory of illness, the instability, that threatens the human soul. The Shaman's personal illness—"the manifestation of a psyche in crisis"—is a sign of election, of superior psychic energy and awareness of dangers in the world. Far from lunatic, the Shaman's so-called "psychomental maladies," tendencies toward morbid sensitivity, taciturnity and meditation, reflect the kind of propitious nervous constitution that provides intimate contact with the spiritual world and the capacity to heal.

On the one hand, the protagonist's idealistic voice encourages him to maintain youthful idealisms: to nurture a drive for awareness, self-possession and moral responsibility, and to pursue dreams of a more just and harmonious social order. On the other hand, the protagonist's lunatic experience breeds a potentially incapacitating despair which undermines his drive for autonomy and social reform. A paralyzing fatalism prompts him to forsake all hope of improvement in the human condition. Hence arises that compulsive search for refuge from life's storms which causes the protagonist to drug himself to reality—to dream dangerous fantasies of perfect peace and harmony which may relieve him from dealing with painful experience, but which threaten to condemn him to the "existential gangrene" spoken of by R.D. Laing. The preface to the novel *Slapstick* establishes that the protagonist's battling voices are indeed Vonnegut's own. Vonnegut identifies the loss of that youthful socialist self who believed in improving labor unions to achieve economic justice. On the other hand, he says that the need to resist the pull of his defeatist self was necessary to life itself. If he is to go on living, he says, he had better follow the lead of idealistic labor leaders like Powers Hapgood.

The problem, then, is that while a majority of critics heed the more audible and visible nihilistic voice in Vonnegut's protagonists—the self filled with "lie down and die"—they miss or ignore altogether its Shaman twin— the efforts of a healthier, yearning, creative self to brave the life struggle, to develop the awareness and courage to act against self-imprisoning cat's cradles and to determine its own spiritual identity in a world of mechanistic conformity and anonymity. Vonnegut's first schizoid hero, Paul Proteus, appears partially successful at best in resisting the system of machines that threatens his sanity. The problem is that despite his inherent resistance to, as he puts it, "carrying out directions from above," Paul ultimately lacks the strength of will and the courage to follow a partially awakened conscience and to act against the totalitarian machinery which he himself helps to administer. As soon as his positive voice asserts itself, the pessimistic voice nullifies it, creating a kind of spiritual stalemate. While we leave Paul Proteus in limbo, the element of hope in Paul's last name, "Proteus," signals a potential for growth realized by future heroes, each of whom becomes increasingly successful in combating defeatism, in struggling against tyrannical systems of control, and in becoming a self-healer and then a healer of others. The denouement to Paul's psychodrama is still to come—not in *Player Piano* and not until the dialectical struggle between hope and despair that begins with Paul is worked out in a process of exorcism and renewal through such extensions of the Vonnegut hero as Malachi Constant, Howard Campbell, Eliot Rosewater, Billy Pilgrim and Kilgore Trout.

Each of these characters is more successful than Paul Proteus in achieving moral awareness and combining this awareness with existential responsibility for his actions. Each confronts the dark side of his personality and attempts to practice the moral imperative described by Malachi's spiritual twin, Unk, in *The Sirens of Titan* as, "making war against the core of his being, against the very nature of being a machine." Yet, tormented by the fear that he is no better than a robot in a machine dominated world, each moves back from the threshold of complete moral awakening that will allow the Shaman to emerge. The lingering pessimism that is Kilgore Trout, or Billy Pilgrim, remains. No resolutions are possible for Vonnegut's protagonists until Vonnegut has found some way to achieve an "equilibrium" based on the belief that people can successfully resist becoming appendages to machines or, as is said of Billy Pilgrim and people in general in *Slaughterhouse-Five*, "the listless playthings of enormous forces."

In opposing the standard view of Vonnegut as fatalist, Kathryn Hume objects as well to the notion that Vonnegut's work is static or repetitious—repeating rather than developing, as Charles Samuels says. Hume sees that Vonnegut's "heavy reliance upon projection makes his books unusually interdependent," "a single tapestry." She infers the spiritual progress of Paul Proteus by noting, "the artistic and personal problems he (Vonnegut) takes up in one story are directly affected by those he did or did not solve in the previous story." Nowhere is Hume's insistence upon the intensely personal nature of Vonnegut's work and upon continuity and progress at the heart of Vonnegut's vision more pertinent than in the case of *Slaughterhouse-Five* and *Breakfast of Champions*—novels Vonnegut says were conceived as one book, and which Peter Reed identifies as the "central traumatic, revelatory, and symbolic moment" of Vonnegut's career.

A striking paradox of *Slaughterhouse-Five* is that it presents us with Vonnegut's most completely demoralized protagonist while making what is to this point the most affirmative statement of Vonnegut's career. The former heroes' gains in awareness and moral courage fail Billy Pilgrim entirely—by design—for Billy like Kilgore Trout in *Breakfast of Champions* becomes Vonnegut's scapegoat, carrying the author's heaviest burden of trauma and despair but whose sacrifice makes possible Vonnegut's own "rebirth." Vonnegut is careful to dissociate himself from Billy as from no character before—signaled by the fact that the author speaks to us directly in the important first chapter about the impact of the war on him, and that with references such as "I was there," and "that was me," he personally turns up in the narrative four times.

In *Breakfast of Champions*, Vonnegut invites us to contemplate a portrait of his more embittered and cynical Trout-self—that "unhappy failure" who represents all the artists who searched for truth and beauty without finding "doodly-squat!" Although Vonnegut happens to be describing his fictional counterpart Kilgore Trout in this instance, their lives are in many ways so similar as depicted in this novel that what is said about the one often applies to the other. Trout is given an iron will to live but a life not worth living. He is given Vonnegut's Shaman-like conscience and artistic goals but a pessimism so great that it negates his artistic mission and vitiates his moral zeal. Trout, in fact, has been turned into a proper Tralfamadorian, believing there is only one way for Earth to be—the way it is. Hence Trout reacts with bitter irony to the coordinator of the Midland City Arts Festival who implores him to bring humanizing new truths and hopeful songs to awake and restore the spiritually dead of his town. "Open your eyes!" exclaims Trout. "Do I look like a dancer, a singer, a man of joy?" Through obvious parallels to Trout, the author tells us that his mounting fear and despair actually made him ill—that his machine-induced nightmares were dreadful enough to result in a state of suppressed schizophrenia that led him to contemplate suicide (his mother's fate) as a solution. He was driven into a void, "my hiding place when I dematerialize," to distance himself from potentially overwhelming horrors. Twin forces of hope and despair were at work in his soul, struggling for control of his creative imagination. But they balanced one another and cancelled one another out, creating a kind of sterile ambivalence, or spiritual stalemate, out of which either irresolution or nihilism emerged as the dominant effect. It was his pessimism that compelled him to fashion the character of Kilgore Trout to bear the brunt of his own cosmic misery and futility. Vonnegut had fractured his own mind, the character Vonnegut tells Trout, and so, for the sake of wholeness, the poisonous Kilgore, the voice of Thanatos, the will to self-destruction, must go. Determining to cleanse and renew himself for the years ahead, Vonnegut sets Trout free, a symbolic act which amounts to the author's repudiation of his most pessimistic voice, and which allows the protagonist's Shaman identity to assert itself. In effect, this constitutes what Eliade calls the "initiatory essence" of the Shaman's preparation for Shamanism—a ritualistic descent into self, a symbolic death and resurrection that transports him into that secret society Vonnegut refers to in *Bluebeard*.

It is on such a healthy note that Vonnegut announces the birth of "a new me," preparing to give us protagonists who not only resist fantasized nirvanas, but who develop the necessary moral sense and faith in human improvement to create for themselves and for others that "humane harmony" lacking in the world around them. We experience the first fruit of the author's spiritual rebirth in his novel *Slapstick; or Lonesome No More*. His subject here is the same—the damaging excesses of the machine upon the human spirit—and he writes of desolated cities and the depletion of nature, of loneliness and spiritual death—but he writes in a voice that is more persistently affirmative than ever before. Dreaming up numerous improvements for mankind, and putting great emphasis on his old idea of the karass from *Cat's Cradle*—bringing together people without great wealth or powerful friends into membership in extended families whose spiritual core is common decency, Vonnegut confirms in this book his optimistic faith that human beings can be anything we want to be. Because people are just families rather than nations, even wars become tolerable; the machines no longer fight and there are no massacres. As Kilgore Trout says in *Breakfast of*

Champions, we are free now to build an unselfish society by devoting "to unselfishness the frenzy we once devoted to gold and to underpants." *Slapstick* bears out that the paranoia that permeates the metafictional writing of the sixties and seventies gradually transforms to more positive forms of fantasy—fabulatory extravaganzas, magic realism. The potentially creative paranoia of Paul Proteus, his stifled gift of invention, gives way to renewal and celebration. The two forms of fantasizing—Paul's and Wilbur's—are contrasted through the desirable social vision of extended families, and the dynamite bouquet represented by Wilbur's delusional visit with a Chinese man the size of his thumb, a dangerous retreat from fear and guilt.

Like Wilbur, the protagonists of *Jailbird*, *Deadeye Dick*, *Galápagos*, *Bluebeard*, and *Hocus Pocus* also become agents of illumination and spiritual healing, characters with restored souls and the creative potency to, as Vonnegut says in the Shaman-like prologue to *Slapstick*, "bargain in good faith with destiny." Each overcomes a crisis of personal identity to become either a literal physician healer like Wilbur, whose work as a pediatrician is symbolically appropriate to curing his own childhood afflictions, or a creator who resolves both personal and social fragmentation by creating fantasies that encourage communal bonding rather than narcissistic withdrawal. There are no Titans or Tralfamadores on the mental horizon of these Shamans, no panaceas or womblike hiding places from complex human problems. Their social visions require no bloody revolutions, no sacrificial messiahs, no deterministic structures and no Godlike figures on whom to thrust moral responsibility. They settle for companionship, fair-mindedness and common decency. With the help of three powerful female guides who personify psychic healing and creative optimism, Walter Starbuck of *Jailbird* fulfills the hero's long frustrated drive for human service as executive vice president of the RAMJAC Corporation, by achieving concrete reforms and putting merciful people in positions of power and influence. Accepting his Shaman-like role, he declares, "I was in an extraordinary position theologically with respect to millions of employees." The redemptive significance of Walter's ascending creative self is conveyed through the wedding gift Walter gives to his wife Ruth, a wood carving of an old person with hands pressed together in prayer. It is, he stresses, a multi-dimensional creation ("my invention") whose attitude of hope and love he himself has designed. The next incarnations of Vonnegut's Shaman hero, Rudy Waltz, Leon Trout, Rabo Karabekian, and Eugene Debs Hartke will move even closer to that final artistic identity by which they merge with their creator, Kurt Vonnegut.

Rudy Waltz of *Deadeye Dick* demonstrates the regenerated hero's creative potency and healing power through his work both as a pharmacist and dramatic artist, learning, as he says, "to be comforted by music of my own making." In a double sense, Rudy, the Waltzer, the scat singer, the writer, becomes his own creator. Climactically the identities of Rudy and Vonnegut connect first in a mirror image of one another and then in the image of an artist-priest with power to raise ghosts from the grave. Eliade tells us that the Shaman is often invited to funerals to prevent the soul of the deceased from returning. Here the function is reversed. In the novel's epilogue, which occurs at the mass grave of those killed by the neutron bombing of Midland City, the gifted metaphysician Hippolyte Paul De Mille offers to raise the ghost of anyone Rudy thinks should haunt Midland City for the next few hundred years. Rudy tells him to go ahead; then he declares, "And I, Rudy Waltz, the William Shakespeare of Midland City, the only serious dramatist ever to live and work there, will now make my own gift to the future, which is a legend."

In *Galápagos*, the work of the protagonist Shaman functions still more purely—as the projective imagination of the Life Force, a directing instrument of the evolutionary process that would help us avoid the kind of sooner-or-later fatal technological horror that occurs in this story. The Shaman now assumes the ultimate role of priest and healer by guiding the destiny of the universe itself. As its title suggests, the setting of *Galápagos* is that of Darwin's *Origin of Species*. With the benefit of nearly a million years of hindsight, the narrator's ghost, which has survived from the year 1986 to the year One Million A.D., tells of "the suicidal mistakes" nations used to make during his lifetime. Suggesting that nature's directions in the year 1986 have been anything but felicitous, the end of life in its present form begins with the introduction of an irreversible disease in which creatures invisible to the naked eye try to eat up all the eggs in human ovaries. Military scientists finish up the job by bringing on an apocalyptic nightmare that changes forever the course of human destiny. Yet, as a welder of human souls as well as ships like the Behia d'Darwin, Leon's evolved will and conscience compels him to complete his research into the human mind and heart, joining ranks with Rudy Waltz to discourage the suicidal impulses of a world verging on absolute sterility and annihilation. Rejecting the fatalism of his father, the noxious Kilgore Trout, Leon achieves the wholeness and the will to declare, "Mother was right, even in the darkest of times, there was still hope for humankind." The mother's optimism informs Leon that mechanistic structures—ticks of the clock such as his father's pessimism, lovelessness and apathy, the stockpiling of weapons of destruction, evolution itself—all are imaginative constructs open to revision. Noting that "The Galápagos Islands could be hell in one moment and heaven in the next. . . ." Leon realizes that it is we who are responsible for our creations, that it is we, as a character says in *God Bless You, Mr. Rosewater*, who "are right now determining whether the space voyage for the next trillion years or so is going to be heaven or hell."

Rabo Karabekian, the hero of *Bluebeard*, represents the main regenerative force in the author's spiritual evolution and the end product of the hero's metamorphosis into the consummate Shaman. It is Rabo, overcoming personal fragmentation to become a healer of others, who asks of his two schizophrenic friends, Paul Slazinger and Circe Berman, "And which patient needed me most now in the dead of night?"

Rabo Karabekian is furthest indeed of all Vonnegut's protagonists from belonging in a prison or asylum. The question of Paul Proteus's sanity posed 50 years ago in *Player Piano* has been answered with an unequivocal assertion of restored mental health. The vigor of Rabo's narrative alone, the energy of Eros, tells us so. But it is the amazing painting in Rabo's potato barn that climaxes and confirms his achievement: a harmony of self and society, body and soul, man and artist, that makes him not only sane but happy— Vonnegut's most emotionally fulfilled hero. At age 71, high time! Soul clap its hands and sing. Rabo subtitle his autobiography "Confessions of an American Late Bloomer"— it might have read, late blooming Shaman—or "Always the Last to Learn."

PETER J. REED

Writer as Character: Kilgore Trout

One of the manifestations of Vonnegut the short story writer that occurs in the novels—as was seen in the previous chapter—is the interjection of stories or other short texts by writers who appear as characters. Various reasons for these inclusions suggest themselves. Most simply, they may assist in the characterization of their authors. On a rather more complex level, when their authors appear as surrogates for Vonnegut himself, or for aspects of him, they may make comment on the writer's craft. Sometimes they do indeed appear to be for light relief, "sending in the clowns," as he puts it. Frequently they are useful for lending another perspective. Particularly in the earlier novels, Vonnegut has been fond of bringing an outside observer onto the scene to provide just such another point of view. The Shah of Bratpuhr in *Player Piano* and the Tralfamadorian Salo in *The Sirens of Titan* serve that purpose. Those two make their observations in the dialogue, but in other instances the commentary comes in written inclusions. They enable Vonnegut to have another voice, in effect. He can say things in a different manner or from a different perspective from that established in the novel's narrative voice. And, importantly for a writer who reaches far in his social commentary, they enable him to get at other topics that may lay beyond the compass of his setting.

Ed, the writer whose wife appears in *Player Piano*, has been mentioned

---

From *The Short Fiction of Kurt Vonnegut* by Peter J. Reed. (Original title: "Other Voices: Kilgore Trout.") © 1997 by Peter J. Reed.

previously. He will not compromise his standards to write what the book clubs want—dog stories or adventure tales. His novels are rejected as too long, too intellectual and too anti-machine. Thus he fails to qualify for the grade of "fiction journeyman," let alone the higher rank of "public relations." Consequently, his wife turns to prostitution, and seems to regard that as a lesser compromise than would be her husband's recourse to popular fiction. Obviously Vonnegut makes fun of his own situation here, since he has been both fiction journeyman and public relations writer at this stage. Even more, however, he takes aim at those who denigrate such honest labor, viewing it as morally on a par with prostitution. The introduction of Ed and his wife into this novel, then, enables Vonnegut to indicate the dangers he sees implicit in the purely commercial dictation of what will be published in an increasingly philistine society. And in the typically two-edged fashion of his satire, he can puncture the elitist "high art" denigration of popular fiction writers.

The central character of *Mother Night*, Howard Campbell, personifies more of the moral ambiguities surrounding the writer. A playwright, he embodies Vonnegut's assertion that people tend to make dramas or fictions of their own lives. He does this first by making a diary of the variety of roles he and his wife Helga invent to keep their sex life vital, called *Memoirs of a Monogamous Casanova*. In time the *Memoirs* become not a diary but a fiction self-consciously created, a real-life drama performed for the writing. Eventually the manuscript is plagiarized and published throughout Eastern Europe, with lurid illustrations, and Campbell feels mortified that the record of his precious love has become pornography. Implicit within this plot are the questions often asked of (and by) writers about their making use of their real life-relationships and acquaintances as fodder for their fiction. More tellingly, perhaps, it parallels the main part of the novel's plot wherein Campbell becomes an American spy and a Nazi propagandist. The fiction he makes of his own life, pretending to be a Nazi propagandist until it becomes hard to say that that is not his primary role, shows the same slide into making the fiction the reality. Hence the moral that Vonnegut says the novel asserts: "We are what we pretend to be, so we must be careful about what we pretend to be."

Campbell writes romantic plays, and his quest for the "authentic hero" makes him unable to resist playing that role himself, hence his acquiescing to become a spy. Looked at less heroically, he cannot resist the role playing, the deception. In the "Editor's Note," Vonnegut writes of Campbell: "To say that he was a writer is to say that the demands of art alone were enough to make him lie, and to lie without seeing any harm in it." But Campbell's lies are not harmless. While he professes that he though the propaganda he writes so ludicrous no one would believe it, people do, and apparently they act on it. That raises the question of what responsibility the writer must assume for people's response to what he or she creates, be it propaganda, public relations copy or fiction. Vonnegut raises that question repeatedly in various guises.

Campbell's role as the central narrative voice makes him the reverse of the outside observers. And yet, Campbell does remain an outsider, a detached observer of the Nazi German scene in which he also participates. This detachment continues in his isolated existence in postwar America, and even in his observations of his guards and fellow prisoners in an Israeli jail. The novel's warnings emerge through both Campbell's detachment and his commentary. His detachment warns of the danger in maintaining an unspoken, inner reservation from the things going on around us. His commentary warns against simplistic and categorical thinking. It rejects equally the bigotry of the neo-Nazi White Christian Minutemen, the popular assumption that Nazis were *different* and went around "trailing slime," and Bernard O'Hare's vengeful conviction he has God on his side. All of this, however, depends upon the intensity of a first person narration and a sustained central role for its full impact. Hence Campbell's dual role.

Writers also occur within *Cat's Cradle*. John, or Jonah, the narrator, embarks upon writing *The Day the World Ended*, which seemingly turns out to be *Cat's Cradle* itself. The other writer is Bokonon, priest-philosopher-charlatan, who writes his *Books of Bokonon*, whose tenets and calypsos are quoted frequently. He declares that all of his truths are *foma*, or shameless if harmless lies, once again raising the issue of the ethics of the writer. Bokonon sums up his philosophy in a calypso that also illustrates his style:

> *I wanted all things*
> *To seem to make some sense*
> *So we all could be happy, yes,*
> *Instead of tense.*
> *And I made up lies*
> *So that they all fit nice,*
> *And I made this sad world*
> *A par-a-dise.*

The Bokononist calypsos and sayings work so well because they are contextualized by a fancifully contrived setting and a charming linguistic environment that includes the Bokononist vocabulary of such things as *wampeters* and *vin-dits* and the San Lorenzan dialect that turns "Twinkle, twinkle, little star" into "Tsvent-kiul, tsvent-kiul, lett-pool store."

Bokonon's functions in this novel are various. In part he serves to underline one of the messages of *Mother Night*, that people are willing to make fictions of their lives and indeed to live by fictions. This novel begins by echoing the opening of Herman Melville's *Moby Dick*, underlining its own fictionality. John announces his intention of writing *The Day the World Ended*, which this novel then depicts. Bokonon, like Campbell, writes fictions that dupe people into behaving in certain ways. That is an aspect of the writer's craft which Vonnegut continues to illustrate with his fictional authors, and to which he sometimes refers directly. In his *Films for the Humanities* interview, for instance, he laughingly points out that just by putting words on a piece of paper a writer can reduce a reader to tears. Here he goes further, the anthropologist Vonnegut showing the willingness of people to believe almost anything and adopt it as a doctrine that makes "this sad world," if not "a par-a-dise," at least "seem to make some sense." That vision, of course, emanates from not just the anthropologist Vonnegut but from the descendant of German free thinkers.

Bokonon's *foma* express the self-conscious fictionality of this book, the self-reflexivity of a text that talks about made-up texts. Its religion's founder, Bokonon, thumbs his nose at his creator, like a character declaring independence of his author. Indeed, Bokonon has made himself up, virtually becoming his own author. Born Lionel Boyd Johnson, he has created his new name, religion, and role. Bokonon and his religion are the vehicles to *Cat's Cradle's* becoming Vonnegut's first truly postmodern novel. Outside of its own fictionality, however, the novel relates to the real world of Haiti, with its "Papa" Monzano a caricature of the actual island's dictator, "Papa Doc" Duvalier, and its religions a parody of symbiosis of Roman Catholicism and Voodoo there. Bokonon remains above all the source of the majority of this novel's humor and breezy irreverence. Like Vonnegut's subsequent favorite writer-character, Kilgore Trout, Bokonon is a debunker, a demystifier, a mocker, an alternative voice through which Vonnegut can find the freedom to be as iconoclastic as he pleases.

The appearance of Kilgore Trout has to await the next novel, however, and *God Bless You, Mr. Rosewater* features another writer-within who should be noted first. This is the disreputable Arthur Garvey Ulm. A struggling writer, Ulm tells the millionaire Eliot Rosewater that he wants to be free to tell the truth, relieved of financial dependence. The ever-naive and hopeful Eliot writes him a huge check on the spot, whereupon Ulm spends eight years only to eventually produce for a book club an eight-hundred pages long pornographic novel called *Get With Child A Mandrake Root*. It begins:

> I twisted her arm until she opened her legs, and she gave a little scream, half joy, half pain (how do you figure a woman?) as I rammed the old avenger home.

Ulm becomes the inverse of *Player Piano*'s Ed, not a writer who refuses to write marketable trash out of economic need, but who does so as an expression of his financial independence. The image of writer reduced to pornographer persists.

In Kilgore Trout the writer becomes reduced to what Vonnegut says the critics regard as *lower* than the pornographer; the science fiction writer. In fact, one of the measures of Trout's low esteem is that his stories are often used as fillers in pornographic publications. Trout varies in his successive incarnations throughout Vonnegut's fiction. His most consistent characteristics are that he writes science fiction stories at an astonishing rate, that he appears a disheveled older man, and that he remains impecunious and generally unknown. Other constants are that he was born in Bermuda, the son of Leo Trout, an ornithologist who studies the Bermuda ern, and that he in turn has a son, also named Leo or Leon. The son has run away and generally despises him, and three marriages have failed, so that he lives alone.

In *God Bless You, Mr. Rosewater*, Trout emerges as the favorite author of Eliot Rosewater, whose praise lavished on science fiction writers has been noted previously. At one point Eliot, obsessed with the polarities of deprivation and wealth he observes, tells a science fiction writers' gathering: "I leave it to you, friends and neighbors, and especially the immortal Kilgore Trout: think about the silly ways money gets passed around now, and then think up better ways." Trout certainly would not be daunted by such a task; his stock in trade is to stand back and take a deconstructive look at something long accepted. His story *2BR02B*, a title Vonnegut had used himself three years previously, sounds like a mix of Vonnegut's plots: it features an America where machines perform all the work, the only people with jobs have three Ph.D.s, there is overpopulation, and Ethical Suicide Parlors stand next to Howard Johnsons. One customer plans to ask God, "What in hell are people *for?*" That question underscores the search reiterated in *God Bless You, Mr. Rosewater* for meaning and substance in the lives of so many.

Another Trout story in *God Bless You, Mr. Rosewater*, recounted by Eliot, is *Oh Say Can You Smell?* It presents a country out to eliminate all odors and conducting research to that end. Finally the country's dictator ends the search at a stroke, not by one chemical to eliminate all odors but by eliminating noses. While essentially a joke, the story also takes aim at the senior Rosewater's conservative politics that seek not to eliminate social inequalities but the sufferers' perceptions of them. Another story, the briefly summarized *The First District Court of Thankyou*, deals with ingratitude. It depicts a court where people could take those they felt had not been properly grateful for a good deed. Those convicted had the choice of thanking the plaintiff publicly or a month in solitary confinement on bread and water.

Eighty percent chose the latter. Recounted in more detail, *Pan-Galactic Three-Day Pass* tells of an interstellar expedition to the outer rim of the Universe. The Tralfamadorian commander of the expedition calls its only human member to tell him he has some bad news from back home. The earthling asks if someone has died. The commander responds, "What's died, my boy, is the Milky Way." Eliot's reading of this story precedes his vision of Indianapolis enveloped in a Dresden-like fire storm. The story has a typical Tralfamadorian distancing perspective, wherein disasters, as can be seen in *Slaughterhouse-Five*, are viewed in the enormous context of all time and space.

Most interesting of the inclusions in *God Bless You, Mr. Rosewater* is Trout's novel *Venus on the Half-shell*. Fred Rosewater furtively picks this off a news stand when he thinks his daughter is not watching, and reads on the back cover "an abridgment of a red-hot scene inside. It went like this:

> Queen Margaret of the planet Shaltoon let her gown fall to the floor. She was wearing nothing underneath. Her high, firm, uncowled bosom was proud and rosy. Her hips and thighs were like an inviting lyre of pure alabaster. They shone so whitely they might have had a light inside. 'Your travels are over, Space Wanderer,' she whispered. . . .

The quotation actually goes on for twenty three lines. After that the back cover photograph of Trout is described as "like a frightened, aging Jesus, whose sentence to crucifixion had been commuted to imprisonment for life." The unique aspect of this passage is that it offers an extended glimpse of a Trout story in his own words.

There is a further point of interest about this story, in that another writer, Philip Jose Farmer, took up this extract and published a novel of the same title using the name Kilgore Trout. In a 1980 interview with Charles Reilly, Vonnegut said this about it:

> *Venus on the Half-Shell* was written by Philip Jose Farmer. . . . I have never met him. He kept calling me up, though, and saying 'Please let me write a Kilgore Trout book.' He was delighted by the character and, as I say, he was a respected writer himself, so I finally said, 'Okay, go ahead.' There was no money involved, by the way; I didn't get a cent of royalties. . . . So he published it, and I wound up getting abuse from all over the place—accusations that I was ripping off college kids' money and whatever.

Later in the same interview, Vonnegut has more to say about what obviously became for him an embarrassing and potentially damaging situation.

> This Farmer wanted to forge on and write a whole series of books 'by' Trout—and I understand he's capable of knocking out a pretty decent Vonnegut book every six weeks. I hardly know Mr. Farmer. I've never met him and most of our contacts have been indirect, so I asked him, please, not to do it. And I asked my publisher, please, not to publish any more of his Trout books because the whole thing had become very upsetting to me. I understand he was really burned up about my decision. I heard he had made more money in that one 'Kilgore Trout year' than he had ever made before—in case you're too polite to ask, I didn't get any of the money.

Thus did the fictional writer almost come to life, as it were, and in something like the kind of confrontation that occurs at the end of *Breakfast of Champions* where a bewildered Kilgore Trout comes face to face with his creator, Kurt Vonnegut. Trout has another fictional meeting with his maker in an interview in *Crawdaddy* for April 1, 1974. This was actually conducted by Greg Mitchell but is set up so as to look as if done by Trout. Vonnegut does acknowledge that Trout has his origins in an actual writer—the science fiction writer Theodore Sturgeon. This was even noted in Sturgeon's obituary in the *New York Times*. "I was so pleased," Vonnegut said, in conversation with Hank Nuwer. "Sturgeon got a nice big obituary in the *Times*, . . . it said in the middle of it that he was the inspiration for the Kurt Vonnegut character Kilgore Trout."

By the end of *God Bless You, Mr. Rosewater*, Trout has been brought in to assist in the recovery of Eliot Rosewater from his breakdown. Charged with putting into words what Eliot has been trying to do, and to establish his sanity, he argues that Eliot had tried to show that people are worth treasuring just because they are human beings, not for what they do or have. He says that Americans, to the contrary, have been trained to hate people who will not or cannot work—including themselves. People need uncritical love, and Eliot has been that rare thing, a person who could give it. The ultimate praise Eliot's father can bestow upon Trout is, "By God, you're great! You should have been a public relations man!" So the marginalized science fiction writer comes to the rescue of the beleaguered saint whose indiscriminate compassion has convinced people of his insanity. It is particularly in these closing scenes of the novel, where Trout assumes the burden of explaining

Eliot's role and hence enunciating the moral message of the book, that he serves Vonnegut best as an alternative voice. Vonnegut avoids the didacticism that would overload another form of direct pronouncement by putting the words in Trout's mouth. Surrounded by comic circumstances and spoken by this undercut figure, the words are relieved of the hard edge of direct statement that might otherwise invite resistance to their import.

In *Slaughterhouse-Five*, Kilgore Trout makes his appearance as the tyrannical supervisor of newspaper delivery boys, a necessary job since he makes no money from his writing. His stories are read, however, and once again by Eliot Rosewater. One of the stories Rosewater reads is *Maniacs in the Fourth Dimension*, about people whose mental illnesses could not be treated because the causes were all in the fourth dimension. Its appeal to the disturbed Rosewater is predictable. He also delights in its claim that vampires, werewolves, goblins and angels all existed, but were in the fourth dimension. "So was William Blake, Rosewater's favorite poet, according to Trout. So were heaven and hell."

The moral of Trout's second story seems more clear, especially in context. Called *The Gutless Wonder*, it tells of a humanoid robot who is despised for his halitosis. The narrator finds the story remarkable for being written in 1932 and predicting napalm. The robot pilots an airplane and drops napalm on people without conscience. Despite this, the curing of his halitosis assures his acceptance into the human race. Bombing people may be socially acceptable, but bad breath never. In the context of this novel with its central event the fire bombing of Dresden, this story's moral is obvious. Once again Trout enables Vonnegut to offer a parable that underlines one of the messages of the novel.

The remaining Trout story in *Slaughterhouse-Five*, *The Gospel from Outer Space*, tells of a visitor from outer space who makes a study of Christianity. In particular he seeks to learn what made it so easy for Christians to be cruel. He concludes the problem lies with careless narration in the Gospels. They were meant to teach mercy, even to the humblest people. They have failed by inviting the interpretation that killing Jesus was wrong because he was "the Son of the Most Powerful Being in the Universe." That leaves the impression that there remain some people it is all right to kill, namely those not well connected. The space visitor leaves Earth a new gospel in which Jesus "really *was* a nobody," though he preached the same philosophy. At his crucifixion God thunders from the sky that he is "adopting the bum as his son," and decrees: *"From this moment on, He will punish horribly anybody who torments a bum who has no connections!"* Here, too, Trout's voice supplements Vonnegut's. This novel depicts the mass slaughter of Dresden, dwells on the horrors of the thirteenth-century Children's

Crusade, recounts one death after another, and chronicles the persecution of the frequently Christ-like Billy Pilgrim. Just as with *God Bless You, Mr. Rosewater*, it is a novel in which a serious, direct statement of the ethics implicit in it would seem didactic and false. Trout's simple, humorous, hyperbolic stories deliver the message effectively without changing the author's narrative stance in the novel.

Breakfast of Champions sees Kilgore Trout being given an even larger role in the novel as a character. As a consequence, a greater number of his stories occurs; more, in fact, than need to be recounted here. Trout makes no copies of the stories he sends off, mostly to "World Classics Library," which uses them to bulk pornographic books and magazines while paying him "doodley-squat." The stories, which usually have no female characters, appear with "salacious pictures" and are often retitled. Hence "Pan Galactic Straw-boss" becomes "Mouth Crazy." It is another over-population story, in which a bachelor produces endless offspring by mixing shavings from his palm with chicken soup and exposing them to cosmic rays. Instead of the society's taking a stand on overly large families, it bans the possession of chicken soup by single people.

"The Dancing Fool" gives vent to some of the frustration Trout-Vonnegut must feel when, Cassandra-like, their warnings go unheeded. Zog, from the planet Margo, comes to Earth to tell humans how to cure cancer and end war. He belongs to a species that communicates by means of tap dancing and farts. As he lands he sees a house on fire and rushes in, tap dancing and farting furiously to warn the occupants. The owner brains him with a golf club. Some plots are simply opportunities for brief comic jibes. In "Hail to the Chief" an "optimistic chimpanzee" becomes President. He wears a blazer with a presidential seal on the pocket. Wherever he goes bands strike up "Hail to the Chief." The chimpanzee is delighted and responds by bouncing up and down.

One summarized plot interests because it appears to prefigure the later novel, *Galápagos*. Trout's novel, *The Smart Bunny*, features a rabbit with the intelligence of Einstein or Shakespeare. She lives like other rabbits so finds her brain useless, regarding it simply as a tumor. She heads for the town to have the tumor removed, only to be shot on the way. The hunter and his wife also concluded that the rabbit has a tumor, is diseased, and therefore do not eat it. In *Galápagos* huge human brains are judged as excessive as the massive antlers of the Irish elk, a creature brought to extinction by over-specialization.

The Trout fiction that has greatest impact in *Breakfast of Champions* remains his novel, *Now It Can Be Told*. The premise of the book is that the reader is the only human; all others are robots, put there by the Creator of the Universe so that he can watch the human's responses. Dwayne Hoover reads this and, taking it as gospel that the robots can neither reason nor feel, dementedly sets off on a rampage. Trout's story splendidly complements major ideas within *Breakfast of Champions*. There are twin themes linked to the notion of people as robots. One envisions people as being robot-like in that they are chemically controlled. This grows out of Vonnegut's own experience in taking anti-depressant pills and discovering that those chemicals can manipulate his mood. The other sees people as being robot-like in the way they are treated. They are made functions of their jobs, doing "women's work," for instance. And often people act as though they shared Dwayne's Trout-induced obsession, viewing the world solipsistically and making other people merely projections of their own visions of reality. Trout's piece of "solipsistic whimsy" makes graphic in its hyperbole the consequences of such attitudes.

In *Breakfast of Champions*, Vonnegut says he is getting rid of all of his characters, and tells Trout he is being set free, leaving him imploring, *"Make me young! Make me young! Make me young!"* But it is not the end of Kilgore Trout. *Jailbird* announces, "Yes—Kilgore Trout is back again. He could not make it on the outside." Once again another writer uses Trout's name. In *Jailbird*, Kilgore Trout becomes one of two pen names used by Dr. Robert Fender. His story "Asleep at the Switch" is recounted at some length. It depicts a large reception center at the Pearly Gates "filled with computers and staffed by people who had been certified public accountants or investment counselors or business managers back on Earth." In a parody of the parable of the talents, these officials give all new arrivals a thorough review of how well they have handled the business opportunities offered them on Earth. Repeatedly they point out each newcomer's missed chances, to the refrain of, "And there you were, asleep at the switch again." The ghost of Albert Einstein emerges as the hero of the story. The auditors tell him that if he had taken a second mortgage and bought uranium commodities before announcing $E=Mc^2$ he could have been a billionaire. And so on. Finally, Einstein gains admittance into heaven carrying his beloved violin. But Einstein recognizes the fallacy in the procedure.

> He calculated that if every person on Earth took full advantage of every opportunity, became a millionaire and then a billionaire and so on, the paper wealth on that one little planet would exceed the worth of all the minerals in the universe in a matter of three months or so.

So Einstein writes God a note, arguing that the auditors must be sadists, misleading new arrivals about their opportunities. God commands an archangel to tell Einstein to be quiet or he will have his violin taken away, and he hushes.

This story obviously parodies the notion of a final accounting, and perhaps also mocks that particular set of preachers who make a large part of their appeal the notion that God *wants* people to get rich. It certainly recognizes the ironic fact that whatever kind of accounting people might expect to make in a next life, a good percentage *act* as if they were to be audited on their financial opportunism. Another point to be made about this story is the way it appears to be triggered simply by the phrase "asleep at the switch again," an expression that seemed to be enjoying a revival at the time. Many of Trout's stories apparently spring from this same kind of spontaneous response to an object, a saying, or a particular event, as also revealed in *Breakfast of Champions.* Trout becomes one of the ways that Vonnegut keeps alive the mischievous, adolescent irreverence, seen in his earliest writing and manifest again and again in his later work, that questions all assumptions and authorities.

One of Fender's other stories, supposedly to appear in *Playboy* under his alternative *nom de plume*, Frank X. Barlow, concerns a planet that runs out of time. Aptly named Vicuna (the animal of that name also may be running out of time), the planet disintegrates as its inhabitants mine time from its very substance. Eventually the Vicunans have to leave their bodies and, like the amphibians of "Unready to Wear," go off as spirits in search of bodies. The central character, a judge, gets to earth. What Vicunans did not realized was that, having entered through the ear of a human, they were unable to leave again. The judge sees what appears to be a happy old man in a quiet place, only to discover he is a criminal in a minimum security prison. The judge finds himself forever locked in the head of a man who aimlessly and interminably repeats a silly scatological childhood rhyme. It seems an apt punishment for a judge who has condemned the convicted to be stood up to their necks in a pond of excrement as deputies aim powerful speedboats at their heads. An interesting detail of this story is that Vicunans say "ting-a-ling" in place of "hello," "good-bye," "please" or "thank you." In a draft manuscript of the later novel, *Timequake*, Kilgore Trout does the same thing.

The Barlow story fits *Jailbird*'s subject matter of trials, convictions and prisoners, but it also relates to this novel's return to that favorite Vonnegut theme of social inequality. Like the Trout story, it underlines the question of the distribution of resources among people. The Vicunans' exhaustion of time itself makes this a parable about human time running out with the exhaustion of resources. That the Vicunans once had bonfires of time when they still regarded it as limitless sends an obvious message about human consumption of things like fossil fuels. The holes that open up in Vicuna as they consume time might be analogous to the holes in Earth's ozone layer.

Perhaps the clearest example of how Vonnegut uses Trout stories as parables, that is allegories or near allegories that illustrate a religious or philosophical moral, occurs in his employment of one called "The Planet Gobblers." Originally cited in a commencement address at Hobart and William Smith Colleges on May 26, 1974, and collected in *Palm Sunday*, the story appears only as summary. In it humans are cast as like "interplanetary termites," who arrive at a planet, use everything up, but always send space ships on to the next planet. They were like a disease, "since it was not necessary to inhabit planets with such horrifying destructiveness. It is easy to take good care of a planet." In his address, Vonnegut quickly goes on to draw out the lesson from Trout's story. "Our grandchildren will surely think of us as the Planet Gobblers. Poorer nations than America think of America as a Planet Gobbler right now." And he goes on to make willingness to change the concluding call of his address.

Kilgore Trout has a major role in the novel *Timequake*, as seen in manuscript form in 1996. His son, whose ghost narrates the novel *Galapagos*, still is depicted as having been killed in a Swedish shipyard in 1975. Since that time, Kilgore Trout has thrown away his handwritten stories within hours of finishing them. He has been writing an average of a story every ten days since he was fourteen, so by the novel's setting of 2000 A.D. he has written about twenty five hundred. He is now an eighty-four-year-old homeless person, one of the "sacred cattle," as he calls them. Like Barlow's Vicunans in the story from *Jailbird*, Trout uses "ting-a-ling" as a general purpose greeting, just one of many echoes in this novel from previous ones.

Another Trout story for *Timequake* is called *The Sisters B-36*. It tells of three sisters, two pleasant and one evil, on a matriarchal planet named Booboo. One good sister paints, the other writes. The third, a scientist, can only talk about thermodynamics, so bores people to death. In an obvious parody of the way people learn and form biases, Trout explains that Booboolings are programmed by what they are told in words when young. Booboolings are thus trained how to look at pictures or respond to ink marks on paper, and develop circuits that Earthlings would call "imagination." So the bad sister, "Nim-nim B-36," invents television. Booboolings no longer need imagination, and only the older ones can appreciate pictures and writing. This makes the two nice sisters feel awful, as she wished, but still no-one likes Nim-nim B-36. So she invents the landmine, barbed wire, the machine gun, the flame-thrower, the computer, and automation. Then Booboolings kill each other readily, feeling nothing because they have no imaginations. "They couldn't do what the old-timers could do, which was see touching stories in faces. So they were unmerciful."

Quite clearly this story speaks, like a parable, to the extraordinary rate at which young people kill each other on American streets. It addresses the vital role that writing and other arts play in the development of the imagination, and the crucial importance of that facility to the culture and the individual. It decries the negative impact that television has had on society. And it returns to two even older themes in Vonnegut's work; pacifism, and the failure of the public to respond with understanding to scientific knowledge. It is vintage Trout, a comic little science fiction story loaded with implication.

Many Trout stories occur in drafts of *Timequake*. In one rather gory tale called *Disgusted Chemicals* various elements lament the horrors societies have inflicted upon the bodies of which they have been part, and come up with a scheme to make all diseases both incurable and fatal. In another, *Bunker Bingo Party*, Hitler pleads, "I never asked to be born in the first place." Trout also leaves an unfinished memoir of the timequake, the central event of this novel, called *My Ten Years on Automatic Pilot*. In one story, ironically told as a lullaby, the crew of a bomber assigned to drop a third atomic bomb, this one on Yokohama, decide not to do it and return to base. At their court martial a fissure opens in the Pacific floor and swallows the island—bomber, crew, courtroom and all. The humor in this story comes in the depiction of the reactions on base as the bomber lands with an atomic bomb slung beneath it giving only eighteen inches clearance from the runway.

Dog's Breakfast tells of a scientist, Dr. Fleon Sunoco, who questions whether the human brain, which he describes as a dog's breakfast or a blood-soaked sponge, is really capable of the greatest human accomplishments. Then he discovers a miniature pink radio receiver in brains taken from extra-intelligent people. He sets about writing up his discovery, convinced he is a cinch for a Nobel Prize. He writes with a fluency he has never known before, until he stops to ask himself where his new-found loquacity, or even his discovery, comes from. It has to be from a receiver in his own brain. He is, in Trout's (or Shakespeare's) words, "hoist by his own petard!" Horrified, Sunoco jumps from the window. Ironically, as a result of his own research, he cannot even be sure that his suicide is his own idea.

Most of the Trout stories in *Timequake* appear only as humorous plot summaries. Two such are *Empire State*, about a meteorite the size of the Empire State Building heading toward Earth, and *Dr. Schadenfreud*, about a psychiatrist who forbids his patients to talk about themselves and who, if they do, will scream, "Who cares about *you*, you piece of shit?" Incidents or phrases from these stories are referred to throughout the novel. Vonnegut uses them to make a joke, to underline a point, or as a kind of refrain.

As in his earlier appearances, Trout supplies *Timequake* with much of its humor and a great deal of its energy. Vonnegut has consistently used Trout's quirky, rapid plots and blunt colloquialisms to inject vitality and pace. They contribute to tone with their often slapstick humor, their outrageousness, and their naive but penetrating observations. Their frequently bizarre science fiction settings help establish mood in novels where Vonnegut unleashes the chaotic to destabilize habitual, unquestioned assumptions about society, the universe, life. From seeming to be a kind of *alter ego* who epitomized what Vonnegut feared he might have become—an unknown hack writer reduced to odd jobs, pornography and ignored science fiction—he has come to embody the questioning mind, the forever adolescent mischief, the irreverent iconoclasm, and the egalitarian conscience that are the quintessence of Vonnegut himself.

DONALD E. MORSE

Thinking Intelligently about Science and Art: *Kurt Vonnegut's* Galápagos *and* Bluebeard

In *Galápagos* (1985) Vonnegut returns for the first time since the phenomenally successful *Slaughterhouse-Five* (1969) to fantasy's "nonidentical twin, science fiction"—but with significant differences between this 1980s extrapolated comic look at the dubious future of mankind and the earlier novels. Gone is the earlier freneticism of *The Sirens of Titan* (1959), the cataclysmic destruction of *Cat's Cradle* (1963), and the predictability of *Player Piano* (1952). Missing also is the Tralfamadorian or God's eye view of all time found in *Slaughterhouse-Five*, and in its place is a sweeping view back to the near future from one million years ahead. Using science fiction and setting the novel a million years in the future becomes in itself, for Vonnegut, "a way of saying God doesn't care what becomes of us, and neither does Nature, so we'd better care. We're all there is to care." This sense of the urgent need to take responsible action now leads Leonard Mustazza to argue that "Ultimately, . . . [*Galápagos*] is not concerned with either the past or the future but the present, is not predictive but cautionary, is not about science or religion but about the way we treat one another here and now." In science fiction, as elsewhere, the future is always a metaphor. In this metaphor used to describe the present, humans appear anything but "lovable," while at the same time Vonnegut intimates that through the use of right thinking and feeling humankind could prevent the ecocide of planet Earth. He maintains

From *Extrapolation* Vol. 38 no. 4 (Winter 1997). © 1997 by Kent State University Press.

that his novel, as contemporary science fiction, "had to be responsible in terms of the theory of evolution, the theory of natural selection . . . [since good science fiction will] make people think intelligently about science and what it can or cannot do. That's what we must do now."

This didactic aim, in part, leads Vonnegut to reject the kind of themes and values found in much of the more traditional science fiction. According to literary historian James Gunn, most if not all science fiction is rooted in the belief that through thinking human beings can indeed save the planet and the species; that through technology a way will be found out of the current ecological dilemma; that progress is not only possible but probable through science; and that, finally, "the farther into space one travels the less significant become the passions and agonies of man, and the only matter of importance in the long morning of man's struggle to survive is his survival so that his sons could be seeded among the stars." Vonnegut says a resounding no! to any such unearthly faith in populating future worlds. Beginning with *Player Piano* and *The Sirens of Titan* and continuing through *Galápagos*—and into the near future novel, *Bluebeard* (1987)—he continually satirizes such absence of values and neglect of the heart necessitated by the shifting of the fictional focus away from individual responsibility to colonizing unknown worlds. Years ago when asked whether he felt there was such a thing as progress—General Electric, for whom he worked for a number of years, used to boast, "Progress Is Our Most Important Product"—or if he thought things were getting better, Vonnegut replied: "I don't have the feeling [that we are going somewhere]." This theme of the lost or never-found sense of direction is present in all of Vonnegut's work, including his future fiction, which helps account for the distopia in *Galápagos*, *Slapstick* (1976), *Slaughterhouse-Five*, *The Sirens of Titan*, and *Player Piano*.

As a novelist, Vonnegut has become increasingly worried about humans destroying the natural world and of the widespread ignorance of nature that encourages such destruction. When faced with a choice between, say, comfort and machine entertainment or some discomfort and an encounter with nature, most characters in his fiction—like most of the Earth's inhabitants—will choose comfort and the machine (see in addition to *Galápagos*, for example, *Player Piano*, "Deer in the Works" in *Welcome to the Monkey House* [1968], or *Breakfast of Champions* [1973]). *Galápagos* itself cautions against this disastrous choice, but unlike many novels that contain a similar warning, including *Slapstick* Vonnegut's weakest novel, *Galápagos* does not postulate an idealized picture of a reversion to some preindustrial state where most of the good things from the contemporary world remain, but society becomes feudal in outlook, organization, and technology. Instead, as Leonard Mustazza observes: "the movement in the narrative [of *Galápagos*] is hi-directional, progressive in that it applies a Darwinian solution to the problem of moral error, retrogressive insofar as the state of innocence that is ultimately achieved is allusively linked to primal mythic innocence." "This was," as the narrator says, "a very innocent planet, except for those great big brains."

The disaster that precipitates the change in evolution in *Galápagos* appears benign, unlike in *Deadeye Dick* (1982), where a neutron bomb wipes out Midland City producing not a murmur from an uncaring, callous, indifferent world; or in *Cat's Cradle* (1963), where human greed and stupidity precipitates death by freezing of all life on the planet; or in *Slaughterhouse-Five*, where the universe ends because a Tralfamadorian test pilot accidentally wipes it out. In *Galápagos* the human population on most of the planet simply fails to reproduce and hence dies out, except for a small saving remnant on the new ark of the Galápagos Islands.

To tell this tale of humanity's evolving "a million years in the future," Vonnegut invents an ideal omniscient, invisible narrator, Leon Trout (son of the nefarious Kilgore Trout), who reads minds, discerns motivation, predicts events accurately over the millennia of his tale. He describes his role as writer as "Nature's experiment with voyeurism, as my father was Nature's experiment with ill-founded self-confidence." Moreover, Leon writes purely for his art's sake, since he has not "the slightest hint that there might actually be a reader somewhere. There isn't one. There can't be one."

The ephemeral nature of Trout's writing along with his total lack of an audience raises issues central to most discussions of contemporary art that Vonnegut explores more fully in *Bluebeard*. They are also cogently posed in Tom Wolfe's story of the masterpiece created by the greatest artist in the history of the world:

> Suppose the greatest artist in the history of the world, impoverished and unknown at the time, had been sitting at a table in the old Automat at Union Square, cadging some free water and hoping to cop a leftover crust of toasted corn muffin . . . and suddenly he got the inspiration for the greatest work of art in the history of the world. Possessing not even so much as a pencil or a burnt match, he dipped his forefinger into the glass of water as his paint. In a matter of seconds . . . the water had diffused through the paper and the grand design vanished, whereupon the greatest artist in the history of the world slumped to the table and died of a broken heart, and the manager came over, and he thought that here was nothing more than a dead wino with a wet napkin. Now, the question is: Would that have been the greatest work of art in the history of the world?

Vonnegut improves on Wolfe's joke while sharpening its point by having his narrator die before he writes *Galápagos* and by having him write on air rather than in water! The result is an invisible novel written by an author dead for a million years.

All of Vonnegut's narrators, including Trout in *Galápagos* and Karabekian in *Bluebeard*, are truly amateur writers, single-book authors with no previous writing experience, which helps account for the "telegraphic . . . manner" that proves as appropriate for the narrators of *Galápagos* and *Bluebeard* to use as it was for the Tralfamadorians in *Slaughterhouse-Five*. Vonnegut has one of his characters in *Bluebeard*, Circe Berman, voice a criticism of Karabekian's style, which echoes many of Vonnegut's own critics: "'How come you never use semicolons?' . . . 'How come you chop it all up into little sections instead of letting it flow and flow?'" But Berman speaks from her own perspective as a best-selling author, unlike Karabekian, Trout fils, or Trout pere, none of whom is concerned about this readership, if any. Moreover, the narrative voice of each—which Vonnegut elsewhere describes as "the voice of a child"— proves admirably suited to their stories and personalities.

In *Galápagos* Vonnegut uses both the fictional technique of an omniscient, if naive, narrator writing in the future for no discernible or possible audience and the startling nature of earth's future fictional inhabitants as ways of commenting satirically on human beings' incredible penchant for self-destruction. The narrator's often incredulous tone, as he observes what humans appear to do best, accentuates what Vonnegut ⟨in *Palm Sunday*⟩ calls "the unbelievability of life as it really is," which in this novel centers on human stupidity, short-sightedness, and unthinking brutality toward one another and the planet. Leon Trout observes from his perspective of "a million years in the future" those large-brained, terribly mobile, inquisitive creatures, whose

> big brains . . . would tell their owners, in effect, "Here is a crazy thing we could actually do, probably, but we would never do it, of course. It's just fun to think about."
>
> And then, as though in trances, the people would really do it—have slaves fight each other to the death in the Colosseum, or burn people alive in the public square for holding opinions which were locally unpopular, or build factories whose only purpose was to kill people in industrial quantities, or to blow up whole cities, and on and on.

The restrained attitude of the narrator nicely mimics that of a doctor diagnosing the illness of a patient. This pose of objectivity becomes in turn a perfect vehicle for satirizing the human mind's delight in devising engines of destruction, such as exploding rockets.

Trout's incredulity also helps emphasize the lack of human foresight that applies thinking not to the problem of survival but to the problem of destruction. Rather than Juvenalian moral outrage, he adopts the more Horacean stance of neutral amazement: "No single human being could claim credit for that rocket, which was going to work so perfectly. It was the collective achievement of all who had ever put their big brains to work on the problem of how to capture and compress the diffuse violence of which nature was capable, and drop it in relatively small packages on their enemies."

Extending this contrast between human creativity and destructiveness, Trout compares the rocket meeting its target with human sexual consummation: "No explosion . . . in Vietnam could compare with what happened when that Peruvian rocket put the tip of its nose, that part of its body most richly supplied with exposed nerve endings, into that Ecuadorian radar dish." Instead of completing the sexual image, Trout breaks the narration to insert an apparently irrelevant comment about art in the far future: "No one is interested in sculpture these days. Who could handle a chisel or a welding torch with their flippers or their mouths?" This violent wrenching away from the sexual imagery used to describe the rocket about to hit its target to the objective statement of the lack of sculpture in the future breaks the narrative flow while pointing to the loss of creativity through violence and sets up the next comic effect by suspending but not abandoning the imagery of sexual consummation. Such imagery contrasts sharply with the rocket's destructive function:

> Into the lava plinth beneath it these words might be incised, expressing the sentiments of all who had had a hand in the design and manufacture and sale and purchase and launch of the rocket, and of all of whom high explosives were a branch of the entertainment industry:
> > . . . 'Tis a consummation Devoutly to be wish'd.
> > William Shakespeare (1564–1616).

Throughout *Galápagos* similar quotations from poets, dramatists, and novelists and from statesmen and philosophers appear juxtaposed to the picture of the downward slide of humanity caused by its failure to listen to the wisdom contained in such quotations or to find value in the creations of its artists. Humans have failed to protect those who love from the effects of war and, worst of all, have insisted on following the path of destruction as exemplified in the rocket's explosive power. Vonnegut's comedy reflects human shortcomings and failures; it warns humanity against approaching disaster, yet does so without moralizing, preaching, or declaiming.

In contrast to *Cat's Cradle*—which apocalyptically concludes with the world coming to an end and which reflects Bokonon's belief that "Maturity . . . is a bitter disappointment for which no remedy exists, unless laughter can be said to remedy anything"—*Galápagos* suggests that laughter and good humor may yet enable humanity to survive the "bitter disappointment" of the inevitable discovery that the word, humanity, and yes, human beings themselves are not only imperfect, but are also an endangered species. When asked on an employment application form what his avocation was, Bokonon wrote "Being alive"; when asked his occupation he wrote: "Being dead." Where *Cat's Cradle* concentrates on human myopia, which chooses the human vocation of death as all life perishes, *Galápagos* emphasize the human "avocation," as the species mutates in order to survive. Rather than the dark apocalyptic humor of *Cat's Cradle*, *Galápagos*'s comedy is lighter and more positive. Brian Aldiss's response to *Galápagos* sums up the novel's strengths: "Sprightly, funny, suspenseful, Candide-like, and endearingly ingenious in its telling"; " . . . the book's a joy" (letter to the author).

Despite its disaster scenario, *Galápagos* has an air of optimism and joy that it shares with *Bluebeard*, which also describes many defeats and short-comings, but of one person rather than the whole of humanity. Rabo Karabekian's mother survived the great massacre of the Armenians by the Turks—which added the word "genocide" to the languages of the world—while her son lives to witness the end of the most destructive war yet fought on European soil when another megalomaniac practiced genocide in his attempt to exterminate systematically a portion of the human race. Yet Karabekian's biography demonstrates that through self-acceptance, and the serious use of imagination and creativity, human beings can become reconciled to their weakness and fragility while still remaining outraged at human stupidity and greed and at the many disastrous self-defeating schemes such "big brained" rational creatures concoct, let alone attempt to implement.

As *Galápagos*, a novel of the far future, examines the misuse of human reason and invention as the principal danger to life on planet earth, so *Bluebeard*, a novel of the near future, looks at the misuse of human creativity as endangering true art. Karabekian, a reformed abstract expressionist painter, is a more complex character in *Bluebeard* than the Rabo Karabekian honored by the Midland Arts Festival for artistic achievement together with the writer-manqué Kilgore Trout (*Breakfast of Champions*). When in the earlier novel Karabekian is challenged by a cocktail waitress to defend his painting The Temptation of St. Anthony, which consisted of a vertical stripe of Day-Glo orange on a field of green as a work of art, he extravagantly replied: "the picture your city owns shows everything about life which truly matters, with nothing left out. It is a picture of the awareness of every animal. It is the immaterial core of every animal—the 'I am' to which all messages are sent. It is all that is alive in any of us—in a mouse, in a deer, in a cocktail waitress. It is unwavering and pure, no matter what preposterous adventure may befall us." Karabekian's speculations parody much of the criticism of abstract expressionism that in a more extreme form appears in Tom Wolfe's spirited, if highly opinionated, book on the necessity of theory for modern art, *The Painted Word* (1975). Although The Temptation of St. Anthony has no content, Karabekian ascribes considerable significance to it: "a sacred picture of St. Anthony alone is one vertical, unwavering band of light. If a cockroach were near him, or a cocktail waitress, the picture would show two such bands of light. Our awareness of all that is alive and maybe sacred in any of us. Everything else about us is dead machinery."

What is striking about Karabekian's defense—besides its articulate self-confidence—what it shares with much of contemporary theorizing about modern art, is the slight, if any, relation these assertions bear to the painting itself. (See, for example, almost any review or essay by the art critic-philosopher Arthur Danto.) Vonnegut satirically suggests that beauty no longer resides in the eye of the beholder, but artistic significance lies wholly within the head of the observer who looks at the painting and theorizes, whether that observer be an artist, critic, or gallery goer.

While this discussion of the nature and value of art is somewhat peripheral to *Breakfast of Champions*, it becomes central to *Bluebeard*. The latter novel raises the perennial issue of what art is and who the "real" artist is by contrasting Karabekian and his abstract expressionist painter friends with Dan Gregory, the illustrator who paints things more real than they appear to the eye, who then lords it over the nonrepresentational painters, who worships Benito Mussolini, and who is "probably the highest paid artist in American history." Examining the abstract expressionists' exuberant splashing of paint on canvas and comparing the astronomical prices they fetch, Vonnegut comments wryly that "Tastes change." Yet Vonnegut's satiric focus is directed only in part to the whimsical nature of the art market. While society makes Gregory fabulously wealthy by purchasing everything he paints, his work fails as art because it has no emotional or spiritual content. Since Gregory's goal is merely to illustrate someone else's ideas or feelings, his work is, although technically proficient, "good painting about nothing," or what Holger Cahill contemptuously calls the "merely decorative."

> . . . art is not merely decorative, a sort of unrelated accompaniment to life. In a genuine sense it should have use; it should be interwoven with the very stuff and texture of human experience, intensifying that experience, making it more profound, rich, clear, and coherent This can be accomplished only if the artist is functioning freely in relation to society, and if society wants what he is able to offer.

Moreover, Gregory's illustrations, although painted in minute and exact detail, are completely removed from "the very stuff and texture of human experience"; they prove as void of content as Rabo Karabekian's extremely well-executed huge abstract canvasses. The novel asks repeatedly which works are art and therefore essential to life and which are decoration and therefore inessential. Are Dan Gregory's fantastic illustrations, Karabekian's wall-sized paintings, or Terry Kitchen's spray-gun paintings valuable as art, or does each have value only as one person's attempt to play with paint? How does each of the three measure up against the great artists of other ages? Can a line be drawn from Rembrandt to Pollock? Or from Gregory to Karabekian? Vonnegut's satire on the world of art, artists, connoisseurs, and critics provides provisional answers. "Artistic justice," for example, occurs in *Bluebeard* when Karabekian's paintings return, "thanks to unforeseen chemical reactions," after a few years to their pristine state as sized canvas: " . . . people who had paid fifteen- or twenty- or even thirty-thousand dollars for a picture . . . found themselves gazing at a blank canvas. All ready for a new picture, and ringlets of colored tapes and what looked like moldy Rice Krispies on the floor." Perhaps Karabekian unwittingly became a conceptualist painter, one whose work exists only as a concept (compare "The Greatest Artist in the History of the World" and Leon Trout's invisible novel), or perhaps he is only the latest example of "Now you see it, now you don't"—as stage magicians used to say during the Great Depression while the rabbit disappeared into the tall silk hat. Or more likely his success illustrates once again the truth articulated in "The Emperor's New Clothes."

Whatever the choice, Vonnegut's satire in *Bluebeard* works because, in addition to its implied and stated criticism, he offers readers a positive standard by which to judge both abstract expressionists and illustrators in Karabekian's final canvas, "Now It's the Women's Turn." This monumental painting records in exact minute detail the moment World War II ended in Europe. Although Karabekian had observed the setting of his painting "when the sun came up the day the Second World War ended in Europe," the meaning, the significance of this event, only revealed itself to him over time (as the meaning or nonmeaning of Dresden unfolded itself over time to Vonnegut). The 5,219 figures in this enormous 64-x-8-foot canvas appear convincingly real not because the artist saw or knew them but because before creating their image on canvas he invented a detailed war story for each, and only after that did he paint "the person it had happened to." His painting is at once as precise as Gregory's illustrations and in some important ways as imaginatively playful as an abstract expressionist canvas.

The painter whose career prompted Vonnegut to create an abstract expressionist proficient in rendering such a scene in great detail was Jackson Pollock, who, according to Vonnegut, did "more than any other human being to make his nation, and especially New York City, the unchallenged center of innovative painting in all this world." Although Pollock spent much of his life dripping paint onto canvas, Vonnegut rightly emphasizes that he "was capable of depicting in photographic detail [any scene desired]. . . . He had been trained in his craft by, among others, that most exacting American master of representational art . . . Thomas Hart Benton."

In "Now It's the Women's Turn" Karabekian returns to "life itself," which he, like most artists of his generation, had ignored "utterly" for very good reasons as Vonnegut notes:

> And could any moralist have called for a more appropriate reaction by painters to World War II, to the death camps and Hiroshima and all the rest of it, than pictures without persons or artifacts, without even allusions to the blessings of Nature? A full moon, after all, had come to be known as a "bomber's moon." Even an orange could suggest a diseased planet, a disgraced humanity, if someone remembered, as many did, that the Commandant of Auschwitz and his wife and children, under the greasy smoke from the ovens, had had good food every day.

But Karabekian goes far beyond this initial reaction. And so with this "last thing I have to give to the world," he discovers and fulfills his vocation as an artist, something he had been unable to do either as an abstract expressionist or as an illustrator. Unlike his earlier work, this last painting reflects powerfully his life experience and feelings. It gives him peace, while eliciting a positive response from the common people who come to view it. He thereby becomes an example of "the artist . . . freely functioning in relation to society, [while] . . . society wants what he is able to offer." No longer does

Karabekian have to browbeat his audience—whether a cocktail waitress in Midland City or his neighbor on Fire Island—into accepting what he has done as art. Rabo the one-eyed painter becomes king in the blind land of art.

Vonnegut intimates in *Bluebeard* that the true artist uses technique—whether it be putting paint on canvas or putting words on paper—to serve human beings and their feelings. Through Karabekian Vonnegut thus aligns himself with, among others, Adolph Gottlieb and Mark Rothko, who challenged the "widely accepted notion among painters that it does not matter what one paints as long as it is well painted. This is the essence of academism." They maintained as a positive alternative that "the subject is crucial and only subject-matter is valid which is tragic and timeless. . . . Consequently, if our work embodies these beliefs it must insult any one who is spiritually attuned to interior decoration; pictures for the home." In the end Karabekian serves humanity not be providing it with more interior or exterior decoration but by depicting a "crucial [subject] . . . which is tragic and timeless." In so doing, he stands out in bold relief against the pale shadow of Dan Gregory, who, despite his talent and popular success, remained merely a "decorator" his whole professional life. Like the notorious Andy Warhol, who once "put an ad in *The Village Voice* saying he would endorse anything, anything at all, for money . . . and listing his telephone number," Gregory wields a brush available for hire; he is ready and able to illustrate or reproduce anything at all for anyone at all for money. In contrast, Karabekian, rather than merely illustrating someone else's idea or feeling, creates something genuine revealing what James Joyce once termed "the simple intuitions which are the tests of reality." His last painting includes all life after the war: the lunatics, war prisoners, concentration camp victims, ragged remnants of an exhausted army, and civilians—the dead, dying, and living. The emphasis falls on all humanity gathered together as the sun comes up after the disaster—"a fair field full of folk," as Piers the plowman said—rather than on the world worn out by war. "Now It's the Women's Turn" and perhaps they will manage things better, intimates Vonnegut at the end of this, his twelfth novel.

Like *Slaughterhouse-Five*, *Bluebeard* concludes with a vision of accepting life as it is, but with a significant difference: if *Slaughterhouse-Five* left the reader with Billy Pilgrim's vision of Tralfamadorian serenity—which by definition is extraterrestrial, and hence unattainable by human beings—*Bluebeard* ends with a picture of the acceptance of human limits, whether of artists, self, friends, or parents. Nor does Karabekian become a "ghost in the rigging" such as Leon Trout in *Galápagos* who is condemned to spend a million years in the Sisyphusean task of recording on air his observations of human beings evolving back to the sea. Instead, he achieves his vocation as an artist, as one who creates a rich portrait of human hope to which others respond enthusiastically. Through Karabekian Vonnegut celebrates human creativity, friendship, and community without which, as shown in *Galápagos*, those "great big brains" would be left on their own to become the ultimate threat to the survival of humanity, of all life, and of the very earth itself. At the end of *Bluebeard* the protagonist, unlike many other Vonnegut heroes, is content and at peace with himself as he celebrates his life and accomplishments saying with all his heart: "Oh happy Meat. Oh, happy Soul. Oh, Happy Rabo Karabekian."

Among Kurt Vonnegut's novels, only *Galápagos* and *Bluebeard*, these nonidentical twins of science fiction and the fantastic, may be said to celebrate life and escape the "air of defeat" that pervades all the others. They also have in common their naive narrators. Although their subjects appear widely separated, the values they espouse are closely related: *Galápagos* warns against the ultimate effects of humanity's proclivity for destroying the planet and all life on it, while *Bluebeard* examines the human temptation to trivialize talent and creativity contrasted with the enduring substance and value of art. In *Galápagos* latter-day human beings slowly evolve over eons into less destructive and far more lovable, furry, polymorphosely perverse, aquatic creatures, thus ensuring their own survival in the far future, along with that of other beings and of the very planet itself. In *Bluebeard* a lone artist in the near future confronting the murderous destructiveness of modern war compassionately transforms its blasted landscape into an image of human hope.

OLIVER W. FERGUSON

History and Story:
Leon Trout's Double Narrative in Galápagos

"How much can you get away with in a book?" Kurt Vonnegut posed
that question in reference to the unorthodox narrative strategy he devised to
solve an "enormous" technical problem that he faced in writing his novel
Galápagos: how to relate, from the perspective of a narrator of our own time,
a story extending from 1986 to one million years into the future.

Galápagos portrays humankind in the year 1,001,986 A.D. and recounts
the circumstances that have led to its condition. As the result of certain
events occurring in the last decades of the twentieth century—worldwide
economic collapse, a destructive war waged by Peru on Ecuador, the global
spread of bacteria that sterilized human females—the only specimens of
humanity in existence are the descendants of a handful of people whose
errant luxury liner ran aground in 1986 on Santa Rosalia, one of the
Galápagos Islands. Thanks to the remoteness of that island, the adaptability
of the small group, and the ingenuity of one of them, humankind escaped the
manmade and natural disasters that eventually destroyed human life
everywhere else; and over time, through the inexorable process of natural
selection, the inhabitants of Santa Rosalia underwent physiological and
behavioral modifications that brought them into perfect harmony with their
environment:

From *Critique* 40, no. 3 (Spring 1999). © 1999 Helen Dwight Reid Educational Foundation.

It was the best fisherfolk who survived in the greatest numbers in the watery environment of the Galápagos Archipelago. Those with hands and feet most like flippers were the best swimmers. Prognathous jaws were better at catching and holding fish than hands could ever be. And any fisherperson, spending more and more time underwater, could surely catch more fish if he or she were more streamlined, more bulletlike— had a smaller skull.

That evolutionary process had other consequences. Because the raison d'être of the Santa Rosalians of a million years hence is to further Nature's goal of ensuring the survival of the species through reproduction, "men and women now become helplessly interested in each other [. . .] only twice a year—or in times of fish shortages, only once a year." And because of their limited cranial capacity, they are not troubled with the "big brains" (the phrase is ubiquitous and unvaryingly sardonic) responsible for the complex totality of human achievement as we know it. In the society of the latter-day Santa Rosalians "nobody [. . .] is going to write Beethoven's Ninth Symphony—or tell a lie, or start a Third World War."

That Darwinian version of the combined New Eden and Noah's Ark myths not only required a plot that unfolded over a million years, but Vonnegut also had to provide a credible point of view for the novel. "The problem was," he remarked in an interview, "who's going to watch for a million years." He solved the problem by creating an omniscient narrator who informs the reader that he is a ghost with the power to assume invisibility and to enter the minds and thereby learn the thoughts and histories of whomever he chooses. Because he is, as he puts it, "Nature's experiment with insatiable voyeurism," he has elected to stay on Earth as a ghost for a million years so that he can see how Nature's experiment with the Santa Rosalians turns out.

The narrator of Vonnegut's evolutionary fable is Leon Trotsky Trout, son of Kilgore Trout, an eccentric writer of science fiction whom readers will recall from some of Vonnegut's earlier novels. Leon is a Vietnam veteran and deserter from the United States Marines who was granted political asylum in Sweden. There, he relates, "I became a welder in a shipyard, [. . . where] I was painlessly decapitated one day by a falling sheet of steel while working [. . . on] the Bahia de Darwin," the vessel that would take the first settlers to Santa Rosalia.

A recent critic has praised Leon as "the perfect vehicle" for the novel, noting that "Vonnegut's boldest experiments in fiction have always been with narrative strategy." A one-million-year-old ghost as narrator is undeniably a bold contrivance. I suggest that Vonnegut's experiment with narrative strategy in *Galápagos* may be even more interesting—and no less bold—than is generally supposed. All of the analyses of the novel with which I am familiar take Leon's assertion of his ghostly nature at face value, tacitly allowing Vonnegut to "get away with" a supernatural solution to his problem. Although such a reading by no means diminishes the impact of the novel, there is another way to regard Vonnegut's narrator, one that relates Leon more intimately to the events in *Galápagos* and that makes him both a more realistic and a more subtly conceived character than the one he professes to be.

Galápagos comprises two narratives: Leon's story—the comparatively detailed record of the Santa Rosalians—and Leon's history—the much briefer, seemingly haphazard account of his life before his metamorphosis. In narrating his history, Leon concentrates on two crucial experiences: his relationship with his family and his military service in Vietnam. Those two experiences are causally related. Leon's parents had diametrically opposed temperaments and attitudes toward life. In their son's succinct characterizations, "my father was Nature's experiment with cynicism, and my mother was Nature's experiment with optimism." Young Leon's naive belief that his father was a great writer led him to become "co-conspirator [. . .] in jeering along with him at Mother," eventually "driving [. . . her] away forever." When he was sixteen he realized that Kilgore Trout was "a repellent failure," a writer of total and deserved obscurity, "an insult to life itself." With that rejection of his remaining parent, Leon also left home, to embark on a fruitless quest to find his mother—and, subconsciously, the father he admired before his disillusionment. His aimless drifting ultimately led him to the Marines and Vietnam.

There is also a significant emotional parallel between Leon's childhood and Vietnam experiences. Each is characterized by enormous feelings of guilt resulting from a traumatic episode. The episode of his childhood is his mother's abandonment of her husband and son and Leon's subsequent rejection of his father; in Vietnam, it is his shooting a Vietnamese grandmother who had killed his best friend with a hand grenade. His emotional response to each is identical. After he shot the Vietnamese woman, he rejected his life as "a meaningless nightmare," wishing he were "a stone at the service of the Natural Order." "The most terrible part of the experience to me," he recalls, "was that I hadn't felt much of anything. [. . .] I hadn't come close to crying. [. . .] I wasn't much for crying even before the Marine Corps made a man out of me. I hadn't even cried when my [. . .] mother had walked out on Father and me."

That confession is made to a Swedish doctor who was treating him for syphilis contracted in Saigon. From Saigon, where Leon was hospitalized for

the "nervous exhaustion" he suffered after he killed the old woman, he was
sent on furlough to Bangkok. There the doctor (eventually responsible for
Leon's flight to Sweden) astonished him by asking if he was related to "the
wonderful science-fiction writer Kilgore Trout." The discovery "that in the
eyes of one person, anyway, my desperately scribbling father had not lived in
vain," moved Leon to "cry like a baby—at last, at last." With the reestablishment of the emotional bond with his father, he now felt something.

The effect of that emotional release was more profound than Leon
realizes: "Father," he explains, "had published more than a hundred books
and a thousand short stories, but in all my travels I met only one person
who had ever heard of him. Encountering such a person after so long a
search was so confusing to me emotionally, that I think I actually went
crazy for a little while." Leon did not go crazy simply "for a little while."
With the return of the emotions repressed since childhood also came the
reawakened consciousness of guilt. To escape the horrors of the present,
Leon took refuge in Sweden; but he could not leave behind his past—with
its accumulated guilt. Unable to cope rationally with his tortured history,
he took refuge in his imagination. Acting not as a stone but as a ghost at
the service of the Natural Order, he denied his corporeal existence and
created a story that envisioned a species to which not only familial life and
human affections but also the common ills of twentieth-century society—
domestic discord, economic free-booting, environmental despoliation, and
war—were unknown.

After completing his lunatic construct, he saw that it was good: "I have
now described almost all of the events and circumstances crucial [. . .] to the
miraculous survival of humankind to the present day. I remember them as
though they were queerly shaped keys to many locked doors, the final door
opening on perfect happiness." That uncritical approval of the life Leon
imagines for the Santa Rosalians—an existence devoid of all the humanizing
aspects of society—is, like Kilgore Trout's wasted career, "an insult to life
itself." And he resembles Kilgore Trout in yet another way:

> And now I catch myself remembering my father when he was
> still alive. [. . .] He was always hoping to sell something to the
> movies. [. . .] but no matter how much he might yearn for a
> movie sale, the crucial scenes in every one of his stories and
> books were events which nobody in his right mind would ever
> want to put into a movie. [. . .] So now I myself am telling a
> story whose crucial scene could never have been included in a
> popular movie of a million years ago.

Leon is not the only character in *Galápagos* who is not "in his right mind." Varying degrees of mental deterioration affect some of the peripheral characters of his story: Roy Hepburn's dementia, Siegfried von Kleist's Huntington's Chorea, and, especially, Giraldo Delgado's paranoia. Significantly, Leon draws a suggestive parallel between himself and that homicidal Ecuadorian soldier: "As to how a person as crazy as Delgado got into the army in the first place: He looked all right and he acted all right when he talked to the recruiting officer, just as I did when I enlisted in the United States Marines."

Readers familiar with Vonnegut will recognize that recurrent motif of mental instability. The two characters from earlier novels who most interestingly resemble Leon are Billy Pilgrim (*Slaughterhouse-Five*) and Eliot Rosewater (*God Bless You, Mr. Rosewater*). Like Leon, they have suffered breakdowns because of traumatic wartime experiences. (The three have an additional point of contact: in *Slaughterhouse-Five* Bill and Eliot meet in a veterans' hospital, where Eliot introduces his fellow-patient to the novels of Kilgore Trout.) The most suggestive similarity between Eliot and Leon is the comparable double burden of guilt that each carries: Leon for rejecting his mother and for shooting the Vietnamese grandmother; Eliot for believing himself responsible for his mother's accidental drowning and for bayoneting a fourteen-year-old German boy.

There is an even more striking parallel between Leon and Billy Pilgrim. One critic has described Billy as "an innocent, sensitive man who encounters so much death and so much evidence of hostility to the human individual [. . .] that he takes refuge in an intense fantasy life." Leon is not the innocent that Billy is (because after World War II innocence is impossible?) and his fantasizing is constant, whereas Billy's is intermittent. For both, however, fantasy is a refuge, a means by which they attempt to cope with a tormented past and an unbearable present. To do that, each performs a radical, though unconscious, manipulation of time.

At random intervals throughout *Slaughterhouse-Five*, Billy comes "unstuck in time." In that mode he is moved arbitrarily from the present moment, "through the full arc of his life," either to a vividly relived episode from his past or to an equally vivid hallucination of a future event. His first experience with that time warp occurred during the war. Later, under the influence of Kilgore Trout's fiction, he comes to believe that he has been kidnapped by aliens from the planet Tralfamadore, where he now lives, making occasional visits to Earth by means of time-travel. That elaboration of his fantasy is Billy's way of providing a philosophical rationale for his time-traveling and of making his remembered past bearable. To the

Tralfamadorians, past, present, and future exist simultaneously. As his captor explains, "[We see] all time as you might see a stretch of the Rocky Mountains. All time is all time. It does not change. [. . .] It simple is." Hence, "when a person dies he only appears to die. He is still very much alive in the past." That conception of time enables Billy not only to endure the memory of the fire-bombing of Dresden but also to deny death its role as a basic fact of the human condition: "Now, when I myself hear that somebody is dead, I simply shrug and say what the Tralfamadorians say about dead people, which is, 'So it goes.'"

Leon's time-travel, unlike Billy's, is unidirectional. His fantasy enables him to know the pasts of the various characters in his story, but after he "comes unstuck in time" in 1986, his concern is with the future—by implication even beyond the year 1,001,986: "Thanks to certain modifications in the design of human beings, I see no reason why the earthling part of the clockwork can't go on ticking forever the way it is ticking now."

Through their manipulation of time, Billy and Leon are able to accept the conditions of their existence. Billy accepts the events of "all-time." Although Leon does not come to terms with the past—his history—quite so satisfactorily, his fantasy—his story—enables him to accommodate to it. By the end of the book, he acknowledges that Nature's successful experiment on Santa Rosalia "almost made me love people just as they were back then, big brains and all."

In his essay on *King Lear*, Harley Granville-Barker observed of the scene in which Lear divides his kingdom, "Its probabilities are neither here nor there. A [. . . writer] may postulate any situation he has the means to interpret, if he will abide by the logic of it after." In following the logic of the postulate that informs *Galápagos*, Vonnegut has provided two equally plausible solutions to the problem of how to contrive a credible plot that must span a million years: the unambiguously supernatural one of Leon as ghost, and the less fanciful but no less ingenious one of him as madman.

Asked how he would grade *Galápagos* (as he had done his previous books in *Palm Sunday*), Vonnegut replied, "In terms of technique I think it's A+. I think technically what I undertook was impossible. I think I solved the technical problems, and it was miraculous to me that I was able to do that." Vonnegut was understandably pleased with his employment of Leon Trout as the narrator of *Galápagos*. Not only is the problem of point of view obviated, but Leon is also useful in other ways. The flashbacks and foreshadowings—as he moves between his story and his history—determine the novel's structure, and his narrative style establishes its tone. And, whether madman or ghost, Leon is the conduit for Vonnegut's criticism of twentieth-century society.

That last function raises the question of the degree to which the narrator of *Galápagos* should be identified with his creator. There are compelling points of resemblance between the two. Both have a common distrust of the benefits of human intelligence: "The human brain," Vonnegut remarked in a 1973 interview, "is too high-powered to have many practical uses in this particular universe," a sentiment echoed by Leon a dozen years later: "The brain is much too big to be practical." Parallels for Leon's mordant observations on contemporary society can be found throughout Vonnegut's fiction; and in the 1973 interview Vonnegut anticipated Leon's brave new world on Santa Rosalia. Deploring the rootlessness and isolation of present-day social structures, he described his "sunny little dream [. . .] of a happier mankind," a dream of the kind of community once found in primitive societies: "I couldn't survive my own pessimism if I didn't have some kind of sunny little dream. [. . .] I want to be with people who don't think at all, so I won't have to think, either. I'm very tired of thinking. It doesn't seem to help very much. [. . .] I'd like to live with alligators, think like an alligator."

Those strong similarities, however, do not warrant reading Leon as Vonnegut's alter ago. As the only reporter of the events of the novel and as an unequivocal critic of contemporary society, Leon necessarily reflects Vonnegut's disapproval of much in that society. As for Vonnegut's yearning for a saurian utopia, we should not be too ready to take it at face value. Hyperbole comes easily for Vonnegut. "You understand, of course, that everything I say is horseshit," he cautioned in the interview. Like his sunny little dream of a life among the alligators, his description of the Santa Rosalian seals is the hyperbolic expression of his anger and despair over the current state of affairs. Leon, it is important to note, is not given to hyperbole. As *Galápagos* abundantly illustrates, his preferred rhetorical figure is meiosis. His approval of the society he describes on Santa Rosalia is consistent and serious. Vonnegut's first novel, *Player Piano*, depicts a nightmarish superstate of the future in which the worship of technology has all but extinguished the human spirit. In the foreword, Vonnegut characterizes it as "not a book about what is, but about what could be." Though he probably did not regard *Galápagos* as a book about what could be, he assuredly did not intend it to represent a way of life that should be.

One critic, who argues that Vonnegut's ostensible desire for a species of humanity unencumbered by a big brain is ironic, compares *Galápagos* to Swift's *Modest Proposal*. A more telling Swiftian parallel is with the fourth book of *Gulliver's Travels*. To satirize the human animal Swift conceived of the houyhnhnms, an equine race of superior beings with none of the vices of mankind. And to maximize the impact of his satire, he employed a naive agent, Lemuel Gulliver, who rejects his own kind and accepts the houyhnhnms as "the perfection of nature." Vonnegut, to express his disgust at the "murderous twentieth-century catastrophes which [. . .] originated entirely in human brains," constructed a fable in which homo sapiens evolves into a race of seal-like creatures incapable of thought, creativity, or mutual destruction. And to intensify the force of his indictment of modern society, he employed Leon Trout, who rejects everything associated with human culture and enthusiastically characterizes the life that has evolved on Santa Rosalia as a condition of "perfect happiness."

Leon is an effective instrument of satire, but his reliability, like Gulliver's, is limited. Both characters have to some extent the qualities they condemn in others. Because of his indiscriminate loathing of humanity, Gulliver is ungrateful to Captain Mendez, his altogether admirable benefactor, and on his return to England treats his wife and children with brutal indifference. Leon's behavior is not so extreme, but he has the besetting folly that he abhors in mankind, "Nature's experiment with [. . .] voyeurism": He chooses to remain a ghost on Earth for a million years to satisfy his curiosity. And though he does not become, as Gulliver does, an object of ridicule, his attitude toward Mary Hepburn's experiment is ridiculously muddled. Mary's "soul," he writes, "[felt] that it would be a tragedy if a child were born" into the inhospitable environment of Santa Rosalia; "but her big brain began to wonder, idly, so as not to spook her," whether the experiment with artificial insemination might possibly work. She did not realize, Leon concludes, that her big brain

> would make her life a hell until she had actually performed that experiment. [. . .] That [. . .] was the most diabolical aspect of those old-time big brains: They would tell their owners, in effect, "Here is a crazy thing we could actually do, probably, but we would never do it, of course. It's just fun to think about." And then, as though in trances, the people would really do it—have slaves fight each other to the death in the Coliseum, or burn people alive in the public square for holding opinions which were locally unpopular, or build factories whose only purpose was to kill people in industrial quantities, or to blow up whole cities, and on and on.

In his deluded admiration for the supposed utopia on Santa Rosalia, Leon is indifferent to the fact that it is the product of humankind's big brain, the origin of everything about modernity that he hates.

In another important way *Galápagos* invites comparison with *Gulliver's Travels*. By separating themselves from the extreme views of their respective narrators, Swift and Vonnegut can achieve the effectiveness of an exaggerated attack on the object of their satire. They can also suggest the possibility of some positive values as a corrective. In the fourth book of *Gulliver's Travels* that hint of something better than Gulliver's distorted vision of humanity is Captain Mendez. In *Galápagos* it is Leon's mother. Leaving her negating husband and son was an act of affirmation. Her favorite quotation (which Leon chooses as the epigraph for his book) is from Anne Frank's diary: "In spite of everything, I still believe people are really good at heart." But because satire is essentially non-celebratory and because Swift and Vonnegut have the temperamental bias toward a pessimistic view of affairs characteristic of the writers of moral satire, those hints of something better are overshadowed. Mendez makes too brief an appearance to offset the terrible yahoos and Gulliver's relentless misanthropy. Anne Frank's poignant expression of faith is vitiated by Leon's complacent application of it to the Santa Rosalians' pointless existence that he so admires: "Mother was right: Even in the darkest time, there really was still hope for humankind." And the symbolic value of Leon's mother—"Nature's experiment with optimism"—is undercut by the bitter ironies of his history: that after a lifetime of searching he never found her; and of his story: that ultimately he comes to identify with his father, Nature's experiment with cynicism: "By golly if I haven't now become a writer, too, scribbling away like Father, without the slightest hint that there might actually be a reader somewhere."

Galápagos, like *Gulliver's Travels*, recognizes the complexity of the human situation. A civilization capable both of producing Beethoven's Ninth Symphony and of destroying itself in a Third World War cannot be dismissed in Leon's simplistic way. That is one part of Vonnegut's message. The other is his unflinching diagnosis of the mortal peril in which humanity finds itself. To convey that, Leon Trout—the mad narrator writing "unsubstantially, with air on air," his desperate fantasy created and made credible by the pressures of his history—is indeed the perfect vehicle for Vonnegut's bleak fable.

Chronology

1922   Kurt Vonnegut born on Armistice Day, November 11, in Indianapolis, Indiana. His grandfather was the first licensed architect in Indiana; his father, Kurt Vonnegut, Sr., is a wealthy architect; his mother, Edith Lieber Vonnegut, is the daughter of a socially prominent family. He has an older brother, Bernard, and a sister, Alice.

1929   With the Great Depression, the family fortune disappears.

1936–40   Attends Shortridge High School where he becomes editor of the *Shortridge Daily Echo*, the first high school daily newspaper in the country.

1940   Enters Cornell University as a chemistry and biology major. Becomes columnist and managing editor of the *Cornell Daily Sun*.

1943   Hospitalized for pneumonia and loses draft deferment; enlists in the United States Army.

1943–44   Studies mechanical engineering at Carnegie Mellon University as part of military training.

1944   Returns home before shipping out; Mother commits suicide by overdosing on sleeping pills, Mother's Day, May 14. Joins 106th Infantry Division; on December 19, Vonnegut becomes German prisoner of war after being captured at Battle of the Bulge. Sent to Dresden, an "open city" presumably not threatened with Allied attack. Works with other POWs in a vitamin-syrup factory.

1945   On February 13–14, U.S. and British air forces firebomb
            Dresden, killing 135,000. Vonnegut and other POWs, quartered
            in the cellar of a slaughterhouse, survive. He later writes that they
            emerged to find "135,000 Hansels and Gretels had been baked
            like gingerbread men." Works as a "corpse miner" in the
            aftermath of the bombing; on May 22, Vonnegut repatriated.
            Marries childhood friend Jane Marie Cox on September 1 and
            moves to Chicago.

1945–47   Studies anthropology at the University of Chicago. Works as
            police reporter for Chicago City News Bureau.

1947   After Master's thesis rejected, moves to Schenectady, New York,
            to work as publicist for General Electric, where his brother
            Bernard is a physicist. Begins writing fiction.

1950   First short story, "Report on the Barnhouse Effect," published in
            Collier's, February 11.

1951   Begins writing full time. Family moves to Wet Barnstable,
            Massachusetts, on Cape Cod.

1952   First novel, *Player Piano*, published; sells short stories to
            magazines, including *Collier's* and the *Saturday Evening Post*.

1953–58   Publishes short stories, works in public relations, runs a Saab
            dealership, teaches English at a school for the emotionally
            disturbed.

1957   Father dies October 1. Sister Alice's husband dies in commuter
            train accident; Alice dies of cancer less than forty-eight hours
            later; the Vonnegut's adopt their three children.

1959   Second novel, *The Sirens of Titan* published.

1961   Collection of stories, *Canary in a Cat House* published.

1962   *Mother Night* published.

1963   *Cat's Cradle* published.

1964   *God Bless You, Mr. Rosewater* published and attracts serious critical
            attention. Begins publishing essays and reviews in *Venture*, the
            New York Times Book Review, *Esquire*, and *Harper's*.

1965–67   Begins two-year residency at the University of Iowa Writers
            Workshop. Novels reissued as paperback editions become popular
            with college students, and attract serious critical attention.

1968   Receives Guggenheim Fellowship; revisits Dresden. A collection
            of short stories, *Welcome to the Monkey House*, published.

1969   *Slaughterhouse-Five; or the Children's Crusade* published and becomes bestseller.

1970   Takes up residence, alone, in New York City; a play, *Happy Birthday, Wanda June*, produced off-Broadway. Serves as Briggs-Copeland Lecturer at Harvard University; Awarded M.A. from University of Chicago: *Cat's Cradle* accepted in lieu of thesis.

1972   *Between Time and Timbuktu* produced for public television; *Slaughterhouse-Five* released as motion picture. Covers Republican National Convention for *Harper's*; elected vice-president of PEN; becomes member of National Institute of Arts and Letters.

1973   *Breakfast of Champions; or Goodbye, Blue Monday!* published; appointed Distinguished Professor on English Prose at the City University of New York.

1974   *Wampeters, Foma, and Granfalloons*, a collection of essays, speeches, and reviews published.

1975   Son Mark publishes *The Eden Express: A Personal Account of Schizophrenia*.

1976   *Slapstick; or Lonesome No More!* published. It is a critical failure.

1979   *Jailbird* published. First marriage ends in divorce; marries photographer Jill Krementz.

1980   A children's book, *Sun Moon Star*, published in collaboration with illustrator Ivan Chermayeff.

1981   *Palm Sunday: An Autobiographical Collage* published.

1982   *Deadeye Dick* published; *Fates Worse than Death* published in England as pamphlet by the Bertrand Russell Peace Foundation.

1985   *Galápagos* published.

1986   Jane Vonnegut Yarmolinsky, his former wife, dies of cancer in December.

1987   *Bluebeard* published. *Angels without Wings: A Courageous Family's Triumph over Tragedy*, by Jane Vonnegut Yarmolinsky, published; it is the story of adopting and raising her sister-in-law's children.

1990   *Hocus Pocus* published.

1991   *Even Worse Than Death: An Autobiographical Collage of the 1980's* published. With wife Jill Krementz, files petition for divorce; it is later withdrawn.

1996   Robert Weide's film adaptation of *Mother Night* is released
        nationally by Fine Line Features. A stage adaptation of
        Slaughterhouse-Five premiers at the Steppenwolf Theatre
        Company in Chicago.

1997   *Timequake* published. Brother Bernard dies.

1999   Film version of *Breakfast of Champions* is distributed in limited
        release.

Contributors

HAROLD BLOOM is Sterling Professor of the Humanities at Yale University and Henry W. and Albert A. Berg Professor of English at the New York University Graduate School. He is the author of over 20 books, including *The Anxiety of Influence* (1973), which sets forth Professor Bloom's provocative theory of the literary relationships between the great writers and their predecessors. His most recent book, *Shakespeare: The Invention of the Human* (1998), was a finalist for the 1998 National Book Award. Professor Bloom is a 1985 MacArthur Foundation Award recipient, served as the Charles Eliot Norton Professor of Poetry at Harvard University in 1987–88, and has received honorary degrees from the universities of Rome and Bologna. In 1999, Professor Bloom received the prestigious American Academy of Arts and Letters Gold Medal for Criticism.

LEONARD MUSTAZZA is co-editor of *Coming After Oprah: Cultural Fallout in the Age of the TV Talk Show* and author of several books, including *Frank Sinatra and Popular Culture*, *The Frank Sinatra Reader*, and *The Critical Response to Kurt Vonnegut*.

JOHN L. SIMONS's essay "Tangled Up in You: A Playful Reading of *Cat's Cradle*" first appeared in *Critical Essays on Kurt Vonnegut* (1990).

CHARLES BERRYMAN is the author of *Decade of Novels: Fiction of the 1970's*, *From Wilderness to Wasteland: The Trial of the Puritan God in the American Imagination*, and *W. B. Yeats: Design of Opposites*.

PETER FREESE is the author of *From Apocalypse to Entropy and Beyond: The Second Law of Thermodynamics in Post-War American Fiction*, *"America," Dream or Nightmare?*, *The Ethnic Detective*, and many articles on American literature and culture.

PHILIP WATTS is Assistant Professor of French at the University of Pittsburgh.

LAWRENCE R. BROER is Professor of English at the University of South Florida. He is the author of *Hemingway's Spanish Tragedy* and *Sanity Plea: Schizophrenia in the Novels of Kurt Vonnegut*, as well as contributor to numerous anthologies of literary criticism.

PETER J. REED is Professor of English at the University of Minnesota. He is author of *Writers for the 70's: Kurt Vonnegut*, and is editor, with Marc Leeds, of *The Vonnegut Chronicles: Interviews and Essays*. His biographical sketches of Vonnegut appear in the *Concise Dictionary of American Literary Biography*, *Dictionary of Literary Biography*, *Magill's Survey of American Literature*, and *Postmodern Fiction: A Bio-Bibliographical Guide*.

DONALD E. MORSE is co-editor of *More Real than Reality: The Fantastic in Irish Literature and the Arts* and *A Small Nation's Contribution to the World: Essays on Anglo-Irish Literature and Language*, and is editor of *The Delegated Intellect: Emersonian Essays on Literature, Science, and Art in Honor of Don Gifford*.

OLIVER W. FERGUSON is the author of *Jonathan Swift in Ireland*.

Bibliography

Allen, William Rodney, ed. *Conversations with Kurt Vonnegut.* Jackson: University Press of Mississippi, 1988.

———. *Understanding Kurt Vonnegut.* Columbia: University of South Carolina Press, 1991.

Bellamy, Joe David, ed. *The New Fiction: Interviews with Innovative American Writers.* Urbana: University of Illinois Press, 1974.

Berryman, Charles. "After the Fall: Kurt Vonnegut," *Critique* 26 (1985): pp. 96–102.

Bradbury, Malcolm. *The Modern American Novel.* New York: Oxford University Press, 1983.

Broer, Lawrence R. *Sanity Plea: Schizophrenia in the Novels of Kurt Vonnegut.* Tuscaloosa: University of Alabama Press, 1994.

Bryan, C. D. B. "Kurt Vonnegut, Head Bokononist," *New York Times Book Review* (6 April 1969): pp. 2, 25.

Burhans, Clinton S., Jr. "Hemingway and Vonnegut: Diminishing Vision in a Dying Age," *Modern Fiction Studies* 21 (1975): pp. 173–91.

Crichton, J. Michael. "Sci-Fi and Vonnegut," *New Republic* 160 (26 April 1969): pp. 33–35.

Gardner, John. *On Moral Fiction.* New York: Basic Books, 1978.

Hartshorne, Thomas L. "From *Catch-22* to *Slaughterhouse-Five:* The Decline of the Political Novel," *South Atlantic Quarterly* 78 (1979): pp. 17–33.

Hassan, Ihab. *Contemporary American Literature.* New York: Ungar, 1974.

———. *Paracriticisms.* Urbana: University of Illinois Press, 1975.

———. *The Postmodern Turn.* Columbus: Ohio State University Press, 1987.

Hearell, Dale. "Vonnegut's Changing Women," *Publications of the Arkansas Philological Association* 22 (Fall 1996): pp. 27–35.

Hendin, Josephine. *Vulnerable People: A View of American Fiction Since 1945*. New York: Oxford University Press, 1978.

Hume, Kathryn. "The Heraclitian Cosmos of Kurt Vonnegut," *Papers on Language and Literature* 18 (1982): pp. 208–24.

———. "Kurt Vonnegut and the Myths and Symbols of Meaning," *Texas Studies in Language and Literature* 24 (1982): pp. 429–47.

———. "Vonnegut's Self-Projections: Symbolic Characters and Symbolic Fiction," *Journal of Narrative Technique* 12 (1982): pp. 177–90.

Irving, John. "Kurt Vonnegut and His Critics," *New Republic* 181 (22 September 1979): pp. 41–49.

Karl, Frederick R. *American Fictions 1940–1980*. New York: Harper and Row, 1983.

Klinkowitz, Jerome. *The American 1960's*. Ames: Iowa State University Press, 1980.

Klinkowitz, Jerome, and Donald L. Lawler, eds. *Vonnegut in America*. New York: Delacorte Press/Seymour Lawrence, 1977.

Lundquist, James. *Kurt Vonnegut*. New York: Ungar, 1976.

Merrill, Robert, and Peter A. Scholl. "Vonnegut's *Slaughterhouse-Five*: The Requirements of Chaos," *Studies in American Fiction* 6 (1978): pp. 65–76.

Morse, Donald E. "Kurt Vonnegut's *Jailbird* and *Deadeye Dick*: Two Studies of Defeat," *Hungarian Studies in English* 22 (1991): pp. 109–19.

———. *Kurt Vonnegut*. San Bernardino, CA: Borgo, 1992.

———. "Kurt Vonnegut: The Antonio Gaudi of Fantastic Fiction," *Centennial Review* 42 (Winter 1998): pp. 173–83.

Mustazza, Leonard. "A Darwinian Eden: Science and Myth in Kurt Vonnegut's *Galapagos*," *Journal of the Fantastic in the Arts* 3 (1991): pp. 55–65.

Olderman, Raymond. *Beyond the Waste Land: The American Novel in the Nineteen-sixties*. New Haven, CT: Yale University Press, 1972.

Pieratt, Asa B., Jr., Julie Huffman-Klinkowitz, and Jerome Klinkowitz, eds. *Kurt Vonnegut: A Comprehensive Bibliography*. Hamden, CT: Shoe String Press/Archon Books, 1987.

Reed, Peter. *Kurt Vonnegut, Jr.* New York: Warner Paperback Library, 1972.

Reed, Peter, and Marc Leeds, eds. *The Vonnegut Chronicles*. Westport, CT: Greenwood Press, 1996.

Scholes, Robert. *The Fabulators*. New York: Oxford University Press, 1967.

———. *Fabulation and Satire*. Urbana: University of Illinois Press, 1979.

Scholl, Peter A. "Vonnegut's Attack upon Christendom," *Newsletter of the Conference in Christianity and Literature* 22 (Fall 1972): pp. 5–11.

Schriber, Mary Sue. "Bringing Chaos to Order: The Novel Tradition and Kurt Vonnegut, Jr.," *Genre* 10 (1977): pp. 283–97.

Uphaus, Robert W. "Expected Meaning in Vonnegut's Dead-End Fiction," *Novel* 8 (1975): pp. 164–75.

Wilson, Loree. "Fiction's Wild Wizard," *Iowa Alumni Review* 19 (June 1966): pp. 10–12.

Acknowledgments

"*The Sirens of Titan* and the 'Paradise Within'" by Leonard Mustazza from *Forever Pursuing Genesis: The Myth of Eden in the Novels of Kurt Vonnegut* by Leonard Mustazza. © 1990 by Associated University Presses, Inc. Reprinted by permission.

"*Das Reich der Zwei:* Art and Love as Miscreations in *Mother Night*" by Leonard Mustazza from *Forever Pursuing Genesis: The Myth of Eden in the Novels of Kurt Vonnegut* by Leonard Mustazza. © 1990 by Associated University Presses, Inc. Reprinted by permission.

"Tangled Up in You: a Playful Reading of *Cat's Cradle*" by John L. Simons from *Critical Essays on Kurt Vonnegut*, edited by Robert Merrill. © 1990 by Robert Merrill. Reprinted by permission.

"Divine Folly and the Miracle of Money in *God Bless You, Mr. Rosewater*" by Leonard Mustazza from *Forever Pursuing Genesis: The Myth of Eden in the Novels of Kurt Vonnegut* by Leonard Mustazza. © 1990 by Associated University Presses, Inc. Reprinted by permission.

"Vonnegut's Comic Persona in *Breakfast of Champions*" by Charles Berryman from *Critical Essays on Kurt Vonnegut*, edited by Robert Merrill. © 1990 by Robert Merrill. Reprinted by permission.

"*Slaughterhouse-Five;* or, How to Storify an Atrocity" by Peter Freese from *Historiographic Metafiction in Modern American and Canadian Literature,* edited by Bernd Engler and Kurt Müller. © 1994 by Ferdinand Schöningh, Paderborn. Reprinted by permission.

"Rewriting History: Céline and Kurt Vonnegut" by Philip Watts from *The South Atlantic Quarterly* 93 no. 2 (Spring 1994): pp. 265–277. © 1994 by Duke University Press. All rights reserved. Reprinted with permission.

"Images of the Shaman in the Works of Kurt Vonnegut" by Lawrence R. Broer from *Dionysus in Literature: Essays on Literary Madness,* edited by Branimir M. Rieger. © 1994 by Bowling Green State University Popular Press. Reprinted by permission.

"Writer as Character: Kilgore Trout" by Peter J. Reed (Original title: "Other Voices: Kilgore Trout") from *The Short Fiction of Kurt Vonnegut* by Peter J. Reed. © 1997 by Peter J. Reed. Reproduced with permission of Greenwood Publishing Group, Inc., Westport, CT.

"Thinking Intelligently about Science and Art: *Galápagos* and *Bluebeard*" by Donald E. Morse from *Extrapolation* 38 no. 4 (Winter 1997): pp. 292–304. © 1997 by Kent State University Press. Reprinted by permission.

"History and Story: Leon Trout's Double Narrative in *Galápagos*" by Oliver W. Ferguson from *Critique* 40 no. 3 (Spring 1999): pp. 230–36. © 1999 Helen Dwight Reid Educational Foundation. Reprinted with permission of the Helen Dwight Reid Educational Foundation. Published by Heldref Publications, 1319 Eighteenth Street, N.W., Washington, D.C. 20036-1802.

Index